DISCOVERING LOVE ONLINE

Love May Be Closer Than You Think

Jonathan,

Thanks for the opportunity to serve on staff at Grace, for your prayers and support and for your testimony and ministry.

Chuck Miller

DISCOVERING LOVE ONLINE
Love May Be Closer Than You Think

CHUCK MILLER

Propeller Cap

INDEPENDENT PUBLISHING
WITH A UNIQUE SPIN

Discovering Love Online: Love May Be Closer Than You Think

Published by Propeller Cap, LLC
Independent Publishing with a Unique Spin
propellercap.com

Copyright © 2018 Chuck Miller

Library of Congress Control Number: 2018932222

ISBN-13: 978-0-9996921-1-0

Cover Design: André Jolicoeur, Doodlemachine
Author Photo: Carol Gregoire, Cherry Blossom Photography

First Edition
Printed in the United States of America

To my winsome bride, Deb, who fills my world with love and laughter; my stepdaughters, Dani and Carol, for making each day more delightful by their presence; and my sister, Janet, a wonderful encourager and friend; and to the memory of my parents, William and Eleanor, who profoundly influenced my life, and my brother, Bill, a kindred spirit and second father. Finally, to singles everywhere who are still seeking the love of their life.

CONTENTS

FOREWORD

F ew relationships influence and shape us more profoundly than those of a romantic nature. Why? Because life is meant to be shared. In the pages you're about to read, Chuck Miller delivers an enlightening and powerful journey of discovery for those entering the world of romance through online dating.

Having recently traveled this road myself, I was impressed by Chuck's insights and observations, as well as his knowledge of resources that I had not considered or that fell into my blind spots. I appreciate the value he delivers in this work. As I read through the manuscript, I often thought, "This would have been helpful to know!" Chuck has done his homework.

Also, since I've known Chuck for a significant part of my life, it's no surprise that he would add value to your search by sharing from his personal losses, gains, first-hand experience and diligent research. His heart in providing this tool is to raise your awareness on many levels as you set out on *Discovering Love Online*.

Chuck assumes nothing as he guides you through the basics and assists you in navigating uncharted territory. He objectively leads you across a landscape of available and powerful resources that are little more than a click or two away. Likewise, though hazards exist on this pathway, some can be bypassed and Chuck is on point to help you avoid those, as well.

Perhaps you've been struggling to overcome self-doubt, limiting beliefs, anxiety or the fear associated with the thought of putting yourself out there. As any coach worth his salt, Chuck helps you assess your level of readiness and challenges you to first "know yourself" before seeking a partner. Would you seriously consider entering a destination into a GPS device while withholding your current location? Unlikely, since both are necessary to plot an effective route. This same principle is true as you chart a course to find the love of your life. Allowing Chuck to guide you through this process will move you in the right direction.

As you begin, consider the time spent mentally and emotionally digesting this content as an investment in your future, both for yourself and for the one longing to be found by you. Isn't that worth the effort?

Love May Be Closer Than You Think!

Brent

Brent Wm. Bauer
Leadership Consultant
Bauer Leadership Consulting Group

PREFACE

T wo years ago, the thought of writing a book about online dating hadn't even crossed my mind. But, life has a way of shaking things up and altering our plans. As a result, you're able to benefit from reading this labor of love on finding love.

Several goals frame the penning of this book. One was to relate my story of seeking and finding love online. A more important objective was to provide you with a means of getting started on a successful search for lasting love yourself. It's not all that difficult when you have the knowledge and tools you need, but still not as simple as pressing a Staples® Easy Button.

GOALS ARE ATTAINABLE

Discovering Love Online: Love May Be Closer Than You Think, and its companion website, began as a project for an entrepreneurial course on product development that I took two years ago. When asked to select my forthcoming creation, several possibilities came to mind. However, it was my wife's proposal to write a book about online dating that seemed to offer the greatest potential, and with good reason.

Prior to my first marriage, I invested over ten years as a young adult in search of love and companionship via traditional dating methods, mostly through my circle of friends and acquaintances. I also gained more than two decades of hands-on experience in the trenches of Christian ministry serving other singles, many engaged in their own search. Recently, as a widower, I concluded a successful adventure-in-online-dating that resulted in marriage to my sweetheart, Deb. All of the above combined to provide a significant vantage point on the topic. That's the abridged version of how this journey began.

Speaking of journeys, everyone embarks on their own dating odyssey with a different skill set, knowledge base and variety of experiences and expectations. Most of you are Internet savvy. Others, not so much. Some may have already dabbled in online dating, while for many it's a new and daunting prospect. A few of you may struggle to navigate the online world and use a computer or other digital device. Either way, it's alright. Life is about extremes and points between.

RESOURCES ARE AVAILABLE

So, regardless of whether you're tech savvy or technologically-challenged, online dating requires a significant investment of time on the Internet. No surprise, right? It's not only your venue for seeking the love of your life, but a repository for many resources to aid in your search. My job is to point you to the best of what's available within and beyond the contents of this book.

In that regard, although I've included hyperlinks[1] to referenced content, they're essentially "permanent" until the book is updated. However, with a perpetually-changing digital landscape, websites close, resources get deleted and URLs[2] change. Meaning, a link that works when I hit the "publish button" may no longer work when you read this book.

As a safeguard to the above, the hyperlinks included in these pages will also appear on the *Discovering Love Online* website in a repository of Online Dating Resources.[3] This will allow me to redirect you to migrated content, delete links that no longer work and add valuable new materials when they become available. So, as you read the following pages, if you come across a "dead" link, please check online.

Another problem with hyperlinks is that they're often long and cumbersome. It's not an issue when linking to Internet content in a digital publication, but a pain when providing links in print. Not only is it difficult to enter longer hyperlinks into your browser, but they're visually grotesque and easy to mistype. As a solution, when a hyperlink is longer than a single line, I've used a link shortener to make it easier for you to copy.

You'll also discover a blog[4] on the companion website where I provide news, articles, reviews, guides and advice to assist you in your search for a future partner. Please check back frequently to access newly-added content. Better yet, subscribe to *Love Notes*,[5] a digital newsletter designed to keep you current on the latest resources added. It will arrive in your inbox at the beginning of each month outlining new content available from *Discovering*

Love Online, along with any promotions being offered in-house or by the online dating services covered here.

If you haven't stumbled across it yet, there's an Internet Dating Survey[6] on the website, as well. Invest a few minutes to take the survey and you'll receive a free gift, a copy of *The Do's and Don'ts of Successful Online Dating*. Preliminary survey results are included in the Appendix of this book.

Finally, *Discovering Love Online* has a home on several popular social media networks. Follow what's happening on Facebook[7] (and join the online community),[8] Instagram[9] and Twitter.[10]

DISCLAIMERS ARE ADVISABLE

As you read this book and navigate the website, you'll discover links to various resources related to online dating. As a matter of full disclosure, I may receive a commission or a portion of sales revenue if you follow one of these affiliate links and make a purchase. Please be advised that such potential remuneration had no influence on editorial content.

While it's my goal to assist you in discovering love online as I did, this book and its website are a business venture. Revenue derived from them allows me to provide ongoing, value-added content to my readers.

ACKNOWLEDGEMENTS ARE IMPORTANT

I'm thankful to everyone who assisted in creating *Discovering Love Online: Love May Be Closer Than You Think*. To my wife and family, kudos for your patience and encouragement during the long process of writing and editing this tome, and for the months involved in developing the companion website. I also appreciate the significant investments made by Deb Miller (the missis), Kathy Schoedler and Karen Shaver in providing editorial feedback that improved the contents of this work. Further, I'm indebted to Brent Bauer, Bauer Leadership Consulting Group,[11] for his perceptive editorial observations and eloquently crafted forward, André Jolicoeur, Doodlemachine,[12] with respect to his delightful cover design, and Carol Gregoire, Cherry Blossom Photography,[13] whose photographic skills made me appear more handsome than usual. And, to eHarmony[14] for providing the mechanism essential to embarking on this journey. Thanks, one and all!

I'm also grateful for a "short commute" to my home office, a cup of tea or coffee to start the day, crispy bacon and scrambled eggs, freshly-brewed iced tea, scrumptious Dove Milk Chocolate Promises, cool Apple tech, comfy slippers, electricity and indoor plumbing. In addition, I'm thankful that this book, and its online counterpart, only required twice as long to create as I had initially envisioned…and not longer.

Last, but only for emphasis, I'm thankful to God for gifting me with the skills and determination necessary to bring this road map to online dating, and its associated website, to life as a resource for singles who long for genuine love and companionship. Thanks to each of you, as well, hopeful readers.

PROLOGUE

B
rett disliked the whole dating scene that was a part of his life from the day he entered high school until he met the woman he married over a decade later. He considered it a necessary evil on the pathway to discovering true love and companionship. Brett found the ordeal of dating disagreeable, emotionally stressful, anxiety inducing and decidedly hit or miss.

He dated enough women over the years to know exactly what he was seeking in a partner and what he wanted to avoid. Still, he found it difficult to meet someone whom he wished to marry who was also interested in marrying him, a woman to share his life with and enrich the years ahead. When Brett and his wife-to-be married, he found great relief knowing that the wearisome dating years were over.

Brianna, as a young adult, also lacked an enthusiasm for dating. It just wasn't a comfortable or enjoyable experience. As in Brett's case, dating was a means to an end and little more. She wanted to get married, but found the process awkward. So, when Brianna finally said, "I do," she bid dating a less-than-fond farewell.

NO GUARANTEES PROVIDED

Regrettably, after 23 years of marriage, and with no children, Brett found himself widowed and alone once again. Since he didn't feel called to the solitary life, nor did he desire it, that meant one thing. Brett needed to re-enter the dreaded "dating zone" in search of companionship. He tried the conventional approach for several years dating women in his circle of acquaintances, but found it stressful and discouraging. Eventually, Brett decided to take advantage of an opportunity previously unavailable and waded cautiously into the uncharted waters of online dating.

Brianna's story was similar. After being married for 30 years, she found herself divorced, single and parenting two teenage girls. Not wanting to resign herself to a life of singleness or to raising her daughters all by herself, she knew the time had come to revisit dating. Since Brianna had a small circle of friends and acquaintances, she determined from the outset that dating online was her best option.

FACE DAUNTING UNCERTAINTY

Brett was familiar with online dating, having seen ads on TV over the years and via the Internet more recently. Services such as eHarmony, ChristianMingle and Match had caught his attention, but most of the stories recounted to him weren't very optimistic. In fact, barring a few couples he knew who had met their spouses online, most of his friends shared "horror stories" of relationships gone wrong or a lack of success in their current search for a lifetime partner—even after spending over a year trying. It seemed too familiar to Brett, conjuring up the same feelings of anxiety and uncertainty that dating produced in the past.

Brianna, likewise, was discouraged by the reports she had heard. Stories it was taking months or years to find someone, of processes that were tediously slow and, in some cases, that no prospective partners were showing an interest. Trying to connect meaningfully was elusive.

APPROACH UNKNOWN TERRITORY

In spite of these uninspiring reports and accompanied by fear and apprehension, Brianna and Brett mustered up the courage needed to venture into the uncertain realm of online dating. Detailed personality questionnaires required over an hour to complete, while online profile creation encompassed several more. It all seemed daunting.

Brett took several days, amid other activities, to wrap up his profile. In the meantime, he became overwhelmed by the number of matches added daily, including many women who wanted to communicate immediately by email or phone. Unprepared for the response, he froze and blocked anyone who seemed too eager to connect. Eventually, he finished his profile, adding photos and answering many of the optional relationship questions. Still, the process took much longer than necessary. Brett just didn't have the knowledge or experience essential to making the endeavor a painless and enjoyable one.

Brianna, nervous about going online in the first place, didn't know what to expect. Assistance needed to fill in her personality questionnaire was unavailable, even through the dating service helpline. She just wanted to create an honest and accurate profile that would produce suitable matches. Yet, those she received didn't seem to match at all. What Brianna needed was knowledgeable assistance in creating her profile. She didn't want to meet a lot of men, just the right one.

FIND ULTIMATE SUCCESS

Eventually, Brett and Brianna learned what they needed to know about online dating. They grew skilled at tweaking their profiles, figured out what to say and the right way to say it, discovered how to eliminate poor matches and concentrate on the most promising ones and acquired firsthand experience in interacting effectively with potential partners.

The good news? Their hard work and diligence paid off! After connecting online and corresponding for several weeks, Brett and Brianna met in person for their first date. Six months later, to the day, they married and began a new life together

TELL A RELATABLE TALE

If your Internet dating experience is similar to that of Brett and Brianna, it's probably not the tale of their success that resonates. Rather, it's with a process that's slow, anxiety ridden and often discouraging. One that's more difficult than it needs to be in your struggle to connect in a meaningful way with a future life partner.

Still, whatever your experience thus far, online dating can be less painful and more promising if you know a few things up front. No secret formulas to master, just a reproducible, step-by-step guide to chaperone you along the path to discovering your Mr. or Mrs. Right—a blueprint to make your dating adventure a positive one with the best possible outcome. That's the purpose of *Discovering Love Online: Love May Be Closer Than You Think.*

Welcome to the adventure!

INTRODUCTION

L ife is filled with unexpected and often undesirable twists and turns, bearing little resemblance to the experience we envisioned for ourselves. If we're honest, many of us are still awaiting the "happily ever after" we expected regarding a life partner. It seems that love has avoided, eluded or abandoned us.

Further, conventional dating methods haven't worked well, or at all, for the majority of singles. I know they didn't serve me well and it's my guess, since you're reading this book, that they haven't been effective for you either. Thankfully, technology introduced an alternative for seeking out the love of our life—online dating.

IT'S NO LONGER TABOO

Once a cultural taboo, Internet dating no longer bears the negative stigma attached to its past. In fact, as of 2017, over 49 million Americans have pursued a relationship online as detailed in a report by Statistic Brain Research Institute,[1] a company dedicated to providing accurate and timely indicators.

According to a study from 2013 published in the *Proceedings of the National Academy of Sciences*, results from nearly 20,000 respondents indicated that over a third of marriages in America had their inception online, a percentage that's likely higher today. Moreover, findings reveal that marriages started online are less prone to result in a break-up when compared with those begun through conventional venues, and they offer a perceivably higher rate of marital satisfaction.[2] That's great news for online daters!

However, depending on your temperament, past experiences and how much of an introvert or extrovert you are—ambiverts, myself included, fall middle-of-the-road—your results with online dating may vary. Some singles will approach it with unbridled excitement, others will experience heart-pounding trepidation. Regardless, a lack of practical knowledge and a host of potential mistakes stand between you and love. In that light, *Discovering Love Online: Love May Be Closer Than You Think* offers you the guidance necessary to stand out among the throng of available prospects. It will help you avoid as many errors as possible while guarding you against sabotaging your own success.

A DIFFERENT PERSPECTIVE MATTERS

Why choose this book over similar titles? Because most lack one critical ingredient: a success story. Many of the books that address online dating have been written by authors who are still single. Of the married writers in the mix, not all met their spouses online. Sadly, others just offer questionable advice, and I'm being kind in this regard. That's why this guide stands in contrast to much of its competition. It emerged from a true "Brett and Brianna" experience. You read the Prologue, didn't you?

Discovering Love Online is different in its viewpoint from most comparable titles, as well. Its aim is to help you find the love of your life, not a one-night stand or passing fling, not someone to engage with socially while you pursue other interests and not just a warm body to date until your soulmate comes along. If that's what you're seeking in a relationship, please look elsewhere. On the other hand, if you want to grow personally, date responsibly and be more productive as you seek out lifelong companionship, you've made a wise investment.

What you have in your hands is also a blueprint based on a Christian worldview, offering guidance in the search for a lifelong, monogamous relationship. Advice shared here applies regardless of your personal experience or religious persuasion, but you need to know the foundation this work is based upon as it's reflected in the pages ahead. Nevertheless, whether you're a person of faith or not, I believe you'll find this resource valuable in your search for true and lasting love.

Finally, *Discovering Love Online: Love May Be Closer Than You Think* is not a catch-all tome comparing conventional dating to its online counterpart. Nor is it an elaboration on every aspect of the Internet dating process. Instead, what you'll discover in the pages ahead are the fundamental steps required to prepare yourself for a successful online dating experience as you search for the love of your life. Presented in a succinct form that's easy to digest and dispensed at a comfortable pace, the information provided here is designed to lead you through a credible process to finding love and companionship online.

SUCCESS IS POSSIBLE

No one can guarantee success when it comes to finding the love of your life, myself included. Even so, steps exist to maximize your online dating experience—things you need to understand in order to replace pain with gain. What many have learned the hard way, by trial and error, you can glean from this book as you prepare to meet that special someone.

Ready? Let's begin!

CHAPTER ONE

START WITH THE BASICS

Dating is about finding out who you are and who others are. If you show up in a masquerade outfit, neither is going to happen.

—*Henry Cloud*

Sam Baldwin, a Chicago-based architect played by actor Tom Hanks, faces a dilemma in the romantic comedy *Sleepless in Seattle*. A year-and-a-half following the death of his wife, Maggie, Hanks' character continues to grieve and struggle with insomnia. Moving to Seattle to escape the reminders of his loss hasn't helped either. Emotionally, he's stuck. Even Sam's eight-year-old son, Jonah, knows his father needs to move on. So, without Sam's knowledge, Jonah phones a national radio talk show and informs America that his dad needs a new wife.

Dubbed "Sleepless in Seattle" by the radio psychiatrist, Sam relates his story on the air, describing his idyllic marriage and how much he still misses Maggie. In the events that follow, including a deluge of letters from would-be suitors, Sam is catapulted back into the world of dating and, as echoed in the signature lyrics of American western entertainer Gene Autry, finds himself "Back in the Saddle Again."

For whatever reason—a death, divorce, break up, time out or fresh start—if you're reading this book, it's apparently time to muster the fortitude to climb back into the saddle yourself and resume dating. Before you do, however, I recommend taking the time necessary to prepare for the experience. Just as you would prior to making any other major decision. As an illustration, you wouldn't invest in the purchase of a new vehicle or home without first reviewing your needs, researching the options available and assessing your financial resources, right? It only makes sense the same should hold true for the weightier decision of entering into a lifelong relationship.

What exactly does that entail? Well, several issues should be considered in advance of seeking a life partner. Regardless of whether you're entering the online dating scene or taking the conventional approach, you need to prepare yourself mentally, emotionally and spiritually for your search. Physically, as well, if you're in poor health or overweight.

You also need to analyze what defines who you are and what you're seeking in a mate. In essence, you need to take a personal inventory. I know the idea can sound a little overwhelming to some of you and like a waste of time to others, but bypassing this step may lead to negative repercussions. So, stick with me. I'll walk you through the process below. But first, I'd like to address the issue of singleness.

CONSIDER THE SINGLE LIFE

While discussing singleness in a book about online dating may initially seem a bit odd, I believe it's valuable in laying a solid foundation for the process of seeking a future companion. So, that's where we'll begin.

First, singleness is not a loss to experience or a sentence to endure, though many view it that way. Rather, it's a stage of life we all experience. Its duration may vary, but we're all single for a season or two as adults—prior to marriage, after the death of a spouse or post-divorce.

Some people actually prefer singleness, enjoying the benefits offered instead of rueing its pitfalls. For them, it's a chosen way of life. But, singleness is not for everyone and the loneliness that attends it can be overwhelming. Still, that's not reason enough to seek escape from the solitary life as it does afford some advantages over being married or involved in a committed relationship. We'll examine just a few.

Singles tend to amass a larger circle of friends and have a more extensive social life than most married couples, along with added time to invest in careers, hobbies, sports and varied interests. I'll offer a personal example. In recent years as a single-again adult, I had over a dozen close friends and a pool of acquaintances in the double digits. At that time, I was involved in a greater number of routine activities and social engagements than at any point during my married years. I interacted with friends a minimum of three times a week, enjoying concerts, movies, county fairs, plays, picnics, potlucks and walks in the park. That didn't even count the occasions I went on dates.

Further, most decisions don't require someone else's input or agreement, making them simpler. Solitude is readily available with fewer distractions and interruptions. And, singles can pretty much do whatever they want whenever they want. Singleness usually, though not always, entails less hardship, as well. As stated in the Bible, "those who marry will face many troubles in this life,"[1] more than those without a spouse and children.

Of course, singleness has its disadvantages, too. As I mentioned previously, being single can be an exceedingly lonely experience, especially among the shy and introverted. That's not uncommon either. In the book of Genesis, God states, "It is not good for the man to be alone."[2] Man being a reference to all mankind, not just men. Life as conceived by our Creator was never meant to be lived in isolation. Companionship is one of our basic needs and, by design, marriage meets that need like no other relationship is capable of doing.

Intimacy is enhanced through marriage, as well. Not just sexual intimacy, although it's a wonderful aspect of a committed, loving relationship, but oneness of spirit, heart and mind. In addition, men and women uniquely complement each other, enabling them to accomplish more together than individually. Marriage also teaches us how to intrinsically put someone else above ourselves. Rearing children does the same.

Moreover, married individuals tend to live longer than their single counterparts, a fact that we've known for quite some time. However, recently collected data has further substantiated this, primarily through a study conducted in 2014 at the NYU Langone Medical Center. Analyzing survey results from over 3.5 million American men and women ranging in age from 21 to 99, it was found that married adults, regardless of age, sex or cardiovascular health, exhibited substantially lower risk factors for heart disease than the participants who were either single, divorced or widowed. According to NYU Langone's senior study investigator and staff cardiologist Jeffrey Berger, M.D., M.S., "Our survey results clearly show that when it comes to cardiovascular disease, marital status does indeed matter."[3]

ACCEPT THE GIFT (OR NOT)

Before moving on, I do want to comment a bit further on marriage vs. singleness as biblically presented, especially as it relates to singles. I know I risk losing some of you at this point, but please bear with me. I'm not going to delve into a prolonged theological discourse on the subject or place a spiritual guilt trip on anyone. Nor am I seeking to convert you to my faith tradition. I simply wish to clarify a misperception that many hold.

It's been my experience over the years that a sizable number of adults, married individuals in particular, have a misconception regarding what the Bible teaches about singleness and relational sufficiency. The Apostle Paul, unmarried himself, remarked in the New Testament that singles can offer "undivided devotion to the Lord"[4] through their "gift" of singleness. He inferred this earlier in the chapter by stating, "I wish that all of you were as I am. But each of you has your own gift from God."[5] Singleness is therefore viewed as a gift given to some, while marriage is considered a blessing presented to others.

I won't discount that last point, as the gift of singleness can be true for all or part of someone's life. I've experienced it myself, twice as an adult. Some truly enjoy the single lifestyle. They're not commitment-phobic. It's just their personal preference. Still, not everyone receives this gift willingly.

Why? I know it goes against the grain of much biblical teaching, but from a relational standpoint singleness comes up wanting. While having a personal relationship with God is an immense blessing and entirely sufficient for anyone's needs, relationally it's not the ideal. Remember, in the Genesis passage I quoted above God clearly indicates that living in a state of "aloneness" is not good for his creation. So, don't feel you're not spiritual enough if you're lonely and want to be married, regardless of what anyone else says. Or, that you're inferior in any way to those who choose to remain single. It's simply the way God designed us.

Nevertheless, it may be preferable for certain people to remain single—for their own benefit and that of a spouse—even though they wish to be married. I'm referring to abusive individuals, those battling severe addictions, as well as the mentally and emotionally challenged. That statement may sound harsh, but placing those single adults in a married relationship could prove to be a recipe for disaster. Clearly, great wisdom is needed for those who desire marriage, yet find themselves in one of the above scenarios.

On a related point, whether you're a Christ follower or belong to another system of belief, questioning the appropriateness or validity of online dating is not unusual. I debated the issue for several months before I finally decided to go ahead and enter the Internet dating arena. My doubts revolved around whether doing so was a sign that I lacked faith in God's provision and was going against his will or if online dating was an allowable option for finding a lifetime partner. In the end, I came to the conclusion that it didn't violate any biblical teachings and that seeking a spouse through the Internet was simply another means God could use in bringing a couple together just as he has, and continues to do, through more traditional dating methods. Considering God's sovereignty, this will come as a freeing statement for many.

In wrapping up our discussion on singleness, you need to decide for yourself if the benefits of marriage sufficiently outweigh the disadvantages of the single life. To most adults, they do. Frankly, you wouldn't be reading this book otherwise.

As a single adult, even though I tended towards introversion, I still developed a large circle of friends and had an active social life. Yet, in spite of that, I often experienced loneliness. Don't get me wrong. I enjoyed my times of solitude. However, when the "party was over" and I was alone once again, I longed to have a companion who held the same values, goals and desires in life.

One last point needs to be shared with regard to singleness. If you're unhappy and lack enjoyment in life as a single adult, don't deceive yourself. Marriage is not a cure-all. You won't suddenly become a happy and fulfilled person by getting hitched. It can add a fresh dimension to your life and bring a new aspect of enjoyment, but it won't change who you are on the inside. When the honeymoon is over and the reality of daily life returns, and it will, you'll still be the same person you were prior to your vows. If you need a change of attitude, attend to that before bringing someone else into your life.

MOVE FORWARD SLOWLY

Since you're still reading, I'll assume that you're seeking marriage over singleness and are eager to pursue online dating. Excellent! The question you need to ask yourself now is, "Am I ready?"

Like you, I sought love and companionship. In my twenties, I was unmarried and lonely. I also believed I was missing out on an important aspect of life. However, it wasn't until my early thirties, while in graduate school, that I met and married my first wife, Millie. Life changed drastically and for the better.

Then, just prior to our twenty-third wedding anniversary, she was diagnosed with terminal cancer and died, and I was faced with a return to marital isolation. Widowed and alone, depression and anxiety moved in as unwanted guests. As a Christian, I knew that "all things work together for good to those who love God"[6] and that I needed to trust him in this loss. Still, that didn't negate my loneliness nor the desire to be married again. Nevertheless, I knew that I needed time to heal before I resumed dating.

A year after being widowed, I began to date again, once every few months for a start. Near the two-year mark, I increased the frequency to once a month, but limited my dating to women in my circle of influence. It was a fair-sized group, as well, since I was a singles director at a large church during that timeframe. Unfortunately, each date ended up being scantly more than an opportunity to rule someone out rather than to find a suitable match. Sad, but true. I also found that the second time around brought with it more baggage that needed to be dealt with than when I had married years earlier. Some of it I carried, but most of it was not my own.

Over the next few years, I dated often. Regrettably, as in the past, the results were disappointing. It was eerily reminiscent of my early years of dating when the Internet didn't exist, a time when conventional dating was the norm. You met someone at work, your place of worship, a social event or some other public setting. Maybe a friend or relative introduced you to "a really great catch" who was just right for you. But, regardless of how you met, almost all dating involved going out with someone who was a complete stranger or a brief acquaintance at best.

EMBRACE NEW OPPORTUNITIES

Thankfully, dating has changed dramatically since those "offline" days and the opportunities for meeting the love of your life are better now than ever. You can still take advantage of conventional dating if you wish, but online dating opens up a whole new world of possibilities. And, more often than not, by the time you go out on a first date you should know a reasonable amount regarding the person you're meeting, enough to eliminate a high percentage of mismatches and those with obvious malicious intent.

A greater knowledge of your potential companion isn't the only difference you'll find between conventional and online dating. With the former, you really don't know the intentions or interests of the person you're asking out or of the one who's asking you out. Are they only "window shopping" or looking for their future spouse? Maybe they're just interested in getting to know you as a friend or seeking someone to spend time with socially. Perhaps, they desire nothing more than a one-night stand.

With online dating, the issue is more clearly defined. Depending on the dating service you choose, intentions and interests can be openly apparent. If not, scrutinizing someone's profile in a little more depth should illuminate the matter. When I signed up on eHarmony, I knew what I wanted and others knew it, too. I was seeking a spouse in no uncertain terms. This concept takes most of the guesswork out of the equation.

TAKE TIME TO HEAL

Before you commence dating online, prior to opening an account and creating a profile, please heed this advice. If you've recently lost a spouse through death or experienced a divorce or a bad breakup, don't rush into a new relationship. Make sure you've taken the time to heal sufficiently beforehand, emotionally in particular. That way you'll be in a healthy, positive frame of heart and mind when you begin.

Unfortunately, I've known several acquaintances who didn't take the time needed to recover first, rushing headlong to replace the love they lost. They married in an attempt to heal themselves, or at least placate their loneliness, rather than addressing the pain first and being ready to date and marry with both wisdom and success. The outcomes were damaging, adding further hurt to individuals already steeped in heartache.

How long does it take for healing to occur? That depends on your circumstances, your ability to deal with loss and the time necessary to work through your pain sufficiently to be healthy again. If you're desperate or needy, you're not ready to date. If you're dealing with unresolved issues and you haven't experienced healing, you may require the assistance of a trained counselor. Another good option for those who have lost a spouse through death or divorce is a recovery program such as DivorceCare,[7] for individuals who experience divorce, and GriefShare,[8] for anyone widowed. Whatever the case, I recommend waiting at least a year before you start to date.

As a final note on healing, I'll share a line taken from Alexander Pope's "An Essay on Criticism." Although its message is directed primarily at the literary critics of his day, the application of Pope's words is appropriate here. "For fools rush in where angels fear to tread."[9] Healing takes time. Don't rush it.

A VOID STILL EXISTS

Another issue I want to comment on relates to needs. Don't be deceived. Your significant other will never fulfill all your needs or even come close. Whether they're mental, emotional, physical or spiritual, it's just not going to happen. So, don't place that burden upon them. Certain needs must be met elsewhere, either within yourself or in God.

Once you've found the love of your life, you'll soon discover, if you haven't already, that a void still exists inside you. One that desperately cries out to be filled. It's a common experience for everyone. Some try to fill it with another person like a spouse, relative or close friend, while others seek to pacify it with alcohol, drugs, cigarettes, food, sex, pornography or some other form of addiction or temporal fulfillment. Unfortunately, those venues all fall short of satisfying the inborn need we have to fill the void of our soul. Those of faith understand why. It's a vacuum that can only be filled by what it was designed to hold in the first place—a relationship with God.

I'm not going to address that God-shaped void in this book other than to draw your attention to its existence and to how it relates to the expectations we place on someone else. Still, it's an important topic that I don't want to gloss over. So, if you wish to learn more about this void and how to fill it, please see the article "Filling the Void of the Soul."[10] You'll find it located on the blog at *Discovering Love Online*. Incidentally, I encourage you to read it before seeking a life partner.

For our purposes, knowing that everyone has a God-shaped void that no one else can fill cautions us against imposing unrealistic expectations on a future spouse. What you need to realize is that no other person is able to fill that emptiness within, not even the love of your life. They can bring you untold happiness and make life more meaningful, but they can't fill a void they were never intended to fill in the first place.

IDENTIFY WHAT DEFINES YOU

I'm not going to wax philosophical, but prior to dating, it's critical to know who you are and what you're seeking in an ideal partner. A phrase that specifically comes to mind is the ancient Greek aphorism, "Know yourself."

Let's look at a few examples to clarify what I'm talking about. If you're a shy, reserved person who enjoys solitude and a quiet evening at home reading a book or watching a movie, choosing to date a guy or gal who's extroverted, prefers hanging with large groups of friends and engages in extreme sports would clearly be a mistake. Your personalities, interests and comfort zones would soon clash. Also, if you come from a conservative upbringing and attend church, temple or synagogue on a regular basis, engaging in a relationship with an atheist, agnostic, cosmic humanist or someone who prefers spending their "day of worship" hunting, fishing, riding their Harley or shopping the sales at the local mall is unwise. That's why you need to clarify who you are before you try and figure out who you're seeking.

How do you accomplish that? Set aside a day and go to a quiet place where you won't be disturbed or distracted. Or, a coffee shop or bistro if that's your preferred environment for thinking. Once you arrive, make a list of your priorities in life, personality traits, significant likes and dislikes, your hobbies and interests, specific personal and relational needs, and the feelings that influence your thoughts, motives and actions. Take your time and don't rush the process. Get it all down on paper or pixels.

You may also want to take at least one of the many personality tests accessible online. Beyond those used by the dating services, available options include the 16 Personalities assessment, Big Five Personality Test, Color Code Personality Test, Keirsey Temperament Sorter and Myers-Briggs Type Indicator. You'll find links to each in the repository of Online Dating Resources at the *Discovering Love Online* website. Many tests are free and can be finished in under 15 minutes. Personally, I recommend that you take several to compare findings, and to complete them in advance of your day away so that you have the results with you.

As you conclude your personal assessment time, make a bullet-point list based on what you've discovered about yourself to use as a guide. This will help you gain a more accurate perspective on who you are and set the stage for determining the type of person you should be pursuing.

QUANTIFY WHO YOU'RE SEEKING

Once you've gained a better understanding of yourself, it's time to establish what you're looking for in a future mate. Make a list of the characteristics you're seeking in a partner before you go online and start setting up your profile. Again, take your time and don't hurry the process.

What should the love of your life bring to the table? Be specific. Jot down everything that comes to mind. You need more than a vague impression. Add this assignment to the agenda for your day of personal clarification or select another time to address it.

Create a list containing the qualities, personality type, physical traits and lifestyle choices that you desire in your special someone and try to be as specific as possible. Are you seeking an introvert, extrovert or ambivert? What age range is preferable? Should they be spontaneous or deliberate? Adventurous or reserved? Do kids fit in the picture? What body types appeal to you? Thin, athletic or fuller figure? How important are religious beliefs? What about marital status? Seeking never-married or widowed singles is usually not an issue for most, but not everyone is interested in a potential partner who's been divorced.

Also, determine in advance what your non-negotiables are in a partner and don't settle for less. You'll only regret it if you do. Will the presence of young children or teenagers in the home be an issue? What about someone who consumes alcohol or smokes cigarettes? Is dating a significant other with addictions in their recent past a tolerable option? Will you accept a companion who has disabilities or health-related conditions? Are you allergic to cats? Do you find big, slobbery dogs a turn off? Know your deal-breakers up front.

In case you hadn't considered it until now, non-negotiables extend beyond the negative traits you're unwilling to accept in a life partner. They encompass positive qualities essential to you, as well. Your list should include qualities such as honesty, integrity, maturity, loyalty, trust, openness, empathy, kindness, optimism, emotional stability, playfulness, dependability, patience, physical affection, humility, respectfulness and financial responsibility. I'm sure you'll think of other positive characteristics to add.

Give due thought to long-distance romances. Are you willing to drive or fly several hours to be with your heart-throb or conduct a significant part of your dating remotely? Apps like Skype and FaceTime help span the gap, but if you develop a long-distance relationship, be prepared to do some traveling. You absolutely need direct encounters to accurately determine if you're a match or not. Establish your stance on this important issue up front, not after you've developed an attachment.

When I created my lists, they formed the basis for who I chose to date, as well as who I excluded from consideration. Once an initial attraction was determined, I would watch carefully for any deal-breakers. Sometimes the non-negotiables were apparent up front, though not in every case. Still, that's one area where Internet dating has a distinct advantage over traditional dating. When you date online, the amount of information available before you end up face-to-face is substantially greater. Thus, awkward moments and wasted time are minimized.

I'll add one caveat. Deal-breakers need to be legitimate. Make sure you don't rule out a potential mate based on a preference as opposed to a non-negotiable. For example, while you may prefer someone who's younger than you, don't miss out on a fabulous partner just because they're a year or two older. It's not that big of a deal. Neither is eye or hair color. Conversely, if you're just not comfortable dating and marrying someone who's taller than you or of the wrong body type, that feeling is unlikely to change, as is the physique of the person in question. Habits and addictions are doubtful to change, as well.

EXHIBIT GOOD BEHAVIOR

As you begin or continue your odyssey in online dating, I have a few behavioral matters to call to your attention. First, if you're a man, prove that chivalry's not dead. Open doors for your date, help her put on her coat and perform other similarly chivalrous acts. Pick up the tab, as well, unless other plans have been made in advance.

Women, you need to let the guy take charge and lead the way in the planning and execution of your date. For instance, if he asks for your input regarding the selection of the restaurant or coffee shop where you'll meet, offer it willingly. Otherwise, defer to him as long as his choices don't compromise your safety in any way. And, assume he'll pay for your meal or other date-related expenses unless he suggests differently.

From a personal standpoint, work at becoming the best "you" possible. In his book *The New Rules for Love, Sex, and Dating*, Andy Stanley recommends making it your goal to become the person that your future spouse is seeking.[11] Self-improvement only betters your chance of attracting the type of individual you want in your life and that someone else wants in theirs. Exhibit gratitude, confidence, assertiveness and friendliness. Focus on helping others, be a good listener and conversationalist (in that order) and be sociable. Moreover, there's no room for selfishness in a committed relationship. If you like having your own way and get upset when that doesn't happen, change or expect conflict.

Also, stop repeating the errors of the past. As an example, if you habitually find dates in bars and they always turn out to be a mistake, stop hanging out in bars. Likewise, when seeking a potential life partner, if their pictures show them partying in clubs what does past experience suggest? If you're not getting the results you desire, quality dates in this case, change your approach to achieve better outcomes. "Doing the same thing, over and over, and expecting a different result" is, by definition, insanity.[12]

Establish standards of conduct in advance, as well, specifically those relating to physical boundaries. The heat of the moment is not the time to determine what's appropriate and what's not. Hormones are exceptionally powerful and you'll almost always exceed the limits that you're comfortable with when passion is aroused. Make sure your date knows your standards, too. Your convictions should be clear from the start, so discuss them early in a relationship. If your prospective partner tries to influence you to compromise your beliefs, bow out and seek someone with convictions that match your own.

LEAVE BAGGAGE BEHIND

Finally, I'd like to comment on several preconceived notions and assumptions about online dating. First, try your best not to bring any baggage into the digital dating sphere, specifically negative experiences and mishaps shared by well-meaning family and friends. Not even any previous exploits you may have had with Internet dating. And, please don't google[13] "online dating horror stories" or you may never log on. Truth is, you'll find just as many disparaging tales to go along with conventional dating.

Don't listen to the naysayers either. Little effort is required to find someone who will gladly advise you to avoid Internet dating, recounting numerous reasons why you should. Usually, they've never tried it themselves, sharing second-hand "facts" about those who did. Then again, maybe they did give it a shot, but weren't prepared for the experience and went about it all wrong.

Honestly, you can find reasons to abstain from anything if you try hard enough. You'll also find just as many reasons, or more, to embark on your own online dating adventure. So, undertake it with an open mind, a well-constructed profile and the necessary precautions, and you should be pleasantly surprised.

In my youth, I was a Boy Scout. Cub Scout and Webelo, too. For those of you who also belonged to the scouts, I'm sure you'll remember the motto, "Be Prepared." It means you're always in a state of readiness, in mind and body, to do the right thing at the right moment. I believe this applies to online dating, too. As you'll discover in the pages ahead, nothing beats being prepared!

Ready to "saddle up" Gene Autry style? In the following chapter, we'll examine the various dating services that make the magic happen and determine where your trail begins.

CHOOSE THE BEST SERVICE

Find a good spouse, you find a good life—and even more:
the favor of God!

—*King Solomon*[1]

N ow that you've gained a better understanding of yourself and what you're seeking in a future partner, it's time to select the best online dating service to achieve your goals. That choice may consist of one service or the combination of several. According to a recent survey conducted by *Consumer Reports* of 9,600 subscribers, 28 percent of those who used more than one site took four or more services for a spin.[2]

Your plan may also encompass an app-based approach. Most of the leading online dating services have a mobile application these days. A handful of popular standalone apps exist, as well, including offerings such as Bumble, Coffee Meets Bagel, Happn, Hinge, Tastebuds and Tinder.

You'll also need to decide whether to use a paid or free service, or possibly combine the two. Both have their pros and cons. In this chapter, I'll address the whole free vs. paid debate and the blur of distinction that's occurring between them. Then, I'll offer some recommendations on services and apps to consider, as well as those to avoid.

FREE IS GOOD...SOMETIMES

The debate between using a free vs. paid online dating service has been raging since the earliest sites first appeared and it shows no signs of abating anytime soon. For many seeking love online, choosing one of the free dating websites seems to make sense. Free is good, isn't it? Well, sometimes it is, but that's not always true. On occasion, free is simply free. I believe it's prudent to heed the old saying, "You get what you pay for," especially when you're seeking a mate.

Still, a blur of distinction has occurred during the past few years between the paid and free alternatives. Many paid-only sites now provide a free, limited-access experience to get you started with the hope of converting you into a paying customer. Services that were once completely-free have added upgrades to improve your dating experience, but taking advantage of those added features comes at a price. Either way, you can get started without making a financial investment.

Irrespective of your choice, one thing holds true with both paid and free alternatives. If you want to enjoy the benefits of premium services along with an enhanced and potentially safer experience, you'll have to pay for it.

PAID IS THE BEST OPTION

While no dating service, paid or free, can guarantee your success, paid sites tend to draw a higher percentage of members looking for a serious, lasting relationship. It should come as no surprise. As with other endeavors, those who make a significant investment of time and money in their online search for love tend to be the most committed to finding success, while cost of entry acts as a buffer for those less dedicated to the process. That's a strong plus in favor of opting for a subscription-based dating service over a free service that offers paid upgrades, since the latter has a blend of members with different commitment levels. Without passing judgment, the clientele on paid services tend to be more earnest in their efforts and more thorough and accurate in creating their profiles. I've experienced it first hand and so have many others seeking love online.

When I began my online search for a lifetime partner, I didn't even consider using a free service. Cost was a secondary factor. Quality and commitment were foremost in my mind. I wanted to find a gal who was just as committed to finding me. My thinking at the time, and still today, was that if someone wasn't willing to make an investment each month to find the love of their life, their commitment level was too low. When you survey the lists that rate online dating services, paid sites normally fill the top five slots and with good reason. That's because they tend to offer a better overall experience and the greatest success rate.

While it may sound like it, I'm not trying to dissuade you from using a free dating service (well, maybe a little). I believe it could prove helpful to employ one in addition to a paid service, though not in place of it. Just be aware that you'll need to invest extra time to weed out poor matches if you do. That's another benefit of a subscription-based service. They assist you in eliminating mismatches or do the job entirely. You end up receiving the best matches for the least amount of effort on your part. Think of it as a pre-screening process.

One other item that paid services normally afford is a greater degree of privacy and safety. In essence, no legitimate credit card on file equals no or limited access to the service by those who would tend to misuse it. Certain sites, eHarmony and Zoosk for instance, offer photo and profile verification services as an added measure of safety.

NOT ALL SITES ARE EQUAL

So, where do you start your search for love? What online dating sites offer the greatest opportunities? Honestly, too many services exist to comment on every one. Estimates vary from hundreds into the thousands, though exact numbers are lacking. In addition to the better-known general-purpose services, a myriad of other sites caters to just about every ethnicity, religion, hobby, interest and sexual leaning imaginable. It can seem overwhelming to make a wise decision due to the diversity of options.

Nonetheless, in most cases I recommend selecting one of the larger, well-known services while avoiding the majority of niche offerings due to questionable practices, lack of safety and privacy, and an extremely limited dating pool. A few exceptions that come to mind include Jdate,[3] a popular dating site for Jewish singles, and CatholicMatch,[4] for those of the Catholic faith.

Given the above, I'm going to focus on the most-popular and trusted alternatives, services that provide excellent value to their members. Don't let that deter you from trying something else if your needs are very specific, but remember that the larger services have extensive member bases and that translates into a greater selection of matches. Plus, I believe you'll find a superior online dating experience sticking to the top-ranked sites.

Some of today's most popular online dating services include, in alphabetical order, Chemistry, ChristianCafe, ChristianMingle, eHarmony, EliteSingles, Match, OkCupid, OurTime, Plenty of Fish and Zoosk. These services consistently receive positive reviews and offer a significant number of monthly visitors. Of course, each site has its strengths and weaknesses, something you need to bear in mind when making your selection. For instance, eHarmony is considered to be one of the best services for marriage-minded individuals, EliteSingles tightly focuses on users with higher levels of education, Match is the 500-pound gorilla offering the largest paid membership and OurTime specializes in helping a 50-and-older clientele find companionship.

How do they compare and which site will serve you best? It really depends on what you prefer in the way of features and user interaction. If you want unrestricted freedom to pour through a voluminous number of profiles and are willing to invest the time it requires, Match could be a good option. If time is an important consideration and you want some of the guesswork eliminated from the equation, eHarmony and EliteSingles both oblige. Looking for a Christian spouse? ChristianCafe, ChristianMingle and eHarmony are appropriate choices. Do you fill a younger demographic? Give Zoosk a try. Older or approaching retirement, OurTime may fit the bill. Just note that sites like Chemistry, Match,

OkCupid, Plenty of Fish and Zoosk also cater to casual daters, not just those looking for a long-term relationship.

I do want to mention at this juncture that the inclusion of a product or service in this book, or on the companion website, should not be construed as a wholehearted endorsement of it. I'm seeking to give you some informed suggestions from which to begin your own search, realizing that everyone's individual likes and dislikes, as well as their needs, differ. To only provide you with my top choices would be a disservice.

Ready to dive in? Great! Let's have a look-in-brief at each of the dating sites mentioned above. Please note that I'm not providing a graded evaluation of these services, but simply a summary to help you choose wisely. Since prices can fluctuate significantly, I won't include that information either. However, links to each service, along with current promotions being offered, are provided on the Online Dating Resources page at the book's companion website.

CHEMISTRY

Created by Match, Chemistry is considered a premium offering, one that employs a unique personality test developed by human behavior expert Dr. Helen Fisher. Its goal is to scientifically provide accurate connections via a matching system based on member preferences and other successful relationships generated through the service. More than 8 million people worldwide have already taken the personality test. Every day Chemistry members are sent personalized matches and given the option to decide if they want to learn more about any of them or not. Self-conducted searches aren't supported, and registration and completion of the personality test take about half an hour.

Pros: Member responses to the matches provided by the service are used to improve future match selections. An extensive personality test is employed, varied tools and games help facilitate interaction between members and privacy is closely-guarded.

Cons: The personality test takes approximately 30 minutes to complete and service pricing is not disclosed until afterward. Very few features are offered compared to other online dating sites, membership is required to view and communicate with other members and a limited dating pool exists, especially in rural areas. Membership auto-renews unless cancelled.

CHRISTIAN CAFE

For those espousing the Christian faith and values, ChristianCafe focuses its efforts on connecting like-minded people and claims over 25,000 marriages to date. Profile creation is quick, just a few minutes. Multiple-choice questions are employed to determine a member's general characteristics while short-answer queries help ascertain spiritual compatibility. Profiles also contain information of specific interest to Christian singles such as denominational background, church involvement, a description of one's faith and favorite Scripture verses. The first ten days of use are free and there's no obligation to upgrade to a paid membership at the end of the trial period. Communication options include email, instant messaging and live chat.

Pros: ChristianCafe is Christian owned with membership geared toward those seeking a marriage partner of faith. Profile searches are both service-provided and member-conducted, and security measures attempt to protect users against loss, misuse and alteration of user data. Member blocking is allowed and a mobile application is available, as well. Communication with other singles is free for ten days and includes sending and receiving email, instant messaging and participating in forums.

Cons: Security measures to protect privacy are undefined, an abundance of search options can potentially reduce compatible matches and a smaller dating pool than other sites limits the number of likeminded partners.

CHRISTIAN MINGLE

Also designed for Christians seeking long-lasting relationships, ChristianMingle allows its 2.4 million members to access their entire database for conducting searches based on denominational preference, age, birthdate, how recently members accessed their profile and other criteria. The service recommends matches each day, as well. User privacy and security are enhanced by manually reviewing every profile and photo to ensure safe, quality matches. Sign-up takes about a minute, allowing access to browse profiles, but additional time is necessary to set match preferences, add photos and complete the subscription process that includes taking a personality test. Smiles and ecards are free to send, but chat and instant messaging require a paid account.

Pros: ChristianMingle was created specifically for those seeking a marriage partner of faith. Members can block other members, a mobile application is provided, pricing is reasonable and an array of communication options exists including smiles, instant messages, email and forums. A decent-size membership is offered by comparison to other faith-oriented sites and solid profiling tools are available.

Cons: Almost too many features exist, photo approval can take anywhere from 24 to 48 hours and a subscription must be cancelled before the deadline or it will auto-renew with no refunds provided. Free trials are available, but with limited features.

EHARMONY

Founded by Dr. Neil Clark Warren, a marriage psychologist who's written numerous books on relationships, eHarmony is a targeted dating service intended for singles seeking a lasting, meaningful connection. It provides extensive compatibility matching for its clientele, removing considerable guesswork from the process. While it can be a little more expensive than other online dating sites, depending on available promotions and the plan selected, it should still rank high on the short list of those seeking marriage, especially anyone coming from a more conservative background. It currently boasts a membership of more than 20 million across 200 countries with roughly 44,000 member weddings annually. Registration requires the completion of an in-depth relationship questionnaire that consists of roughly 150 queries (reduced from over 450). Once registered, eHarmony sends new members their first round of potential matches.

Pros: eHarmony offers an industry-leading compatibility test and excellent Guided Communication options for its members that include pre-selected Quick Questions, a Makes or Breaks list, personalized Dig Deeper queries, eH Mail (internal email system) and SecureCall for secure, anonymous calling. RelyID allows members to verify their identity for added security, a mobile app is provided, solid dating advice and resources are incorporated, and those separated from their spouse are prohibited from joining, a benefit that few online dating services provide. eHarmony now offers free accounts with limited features.

Cons: The service is a little expensive compared to most others apart from special promotions, matching features incorporated are less "fun" than what's provided by its competition, and individual browsing and searching are not supported. eHarmony supplies all matches (viewed as a plus by many members). The compatibility pool, while respectable, is less extensive than other popular sites.

ELITE SINGLES

Fashioned for those seeking a serious relationship, EliteSingles offers its clientele guided communication and manually verifies each new profile to help provide its users with a safe, enjoyable experience. The site attracts educated professionals, with over 80 percent of its members possessing a bachelor's degree or higher. Matches are based on a combination of the Five Factor Model personality test (conscientiousness, neuroticism, agreeableness, extraversion and openness) plus an individual's specific search preferences. To register, users provide basic profile data, complete the extensive personality test and enter relationship search criteria including preferred age, desire for children and distance radius. Once complete, EliteSingles supplies three to seven compatible matches daily to its members. If that's insufficient, adding a paid upgrade increases the number by as much as 20 more per day.

Pros: Security is a priority employing ID authentication, fraud detection and manual profile verification. Exclusive singles events are offered to its members, a mobile app is available and correspondence options include ice-breaker questions, smiles and email. Users can register, take the personality test, create a profile and receive specific partner suggestions without charge, although payment is required to communicate with potential matches.

Cons: Registration is time consuming, user searches are not supported, limited matches are suggested per day and chat features are unavailable. EliteSingles is also one of the more expensive dating services.

MATCH

One of the largest online dating services in the world with around 30 million members, Match offers some of the most extensive features and communication options available. It provides site-generated matching and self-conducted searches, testimonials from friends and family, assistance creating profiles (for an added charge), organization of all correspondence, international dating, local Match-sponsored events, live chat and tools to narrow your searches. While browsing is free, registration is required before being matched. A somewhat lengthy questionnaire employed to improve matching accuracy is followed up by a waiting period of up to a day before your profile is approved.

Pros: Match guarantees its paid members an additional six months of membership free if they don't find a meaningful connection during their first six. Excellent search features are incorporated, members can view profiles incognito, a personal email account is provided, valuable dating tips and resources are available, and friends on the service can suggest their own matches for each other. Communication options include winks, emails and instant messaging. A mobile application is also offered.

Cons: Profile creation can be time-consuming and the service is as much—if not more—a site for casual dating than it is for finding serious relationships. Only paying members can communicate, pricing is on the high-end and subscriptions renew automatically unless an account is cancelled before the next billing cycle.

OK CUPID

OkCupid is one of the most popular free online dating services around. It offers a solid matching engine with searches based on criteria such as age, location and dating expectations. Serving a clientele that leans toward creative types, it provides fun quizzes and ice breakers allowing members to interact with both potential matches and to the overall dating community. Sign-up requires minimal effort. However, once registered, new users need to fill in basic information such as body type, distance and ethnicity, as well as complete a series of "yes" or "no" questions that are used to determine compatibility.

Pros: Users can search and communicate for free and a compatibility percentage is offered for each match along with how it was determined. The profile questions posed allow members to indicate their importance and value, good privacy features are integrated and a mobile app provides access on the go.

Cons: Annoying site ads appear unless a paid option is selected, invisible browsing is not supported without a paid membership and its matching pool is smaller than other sites, specifically in rural areas. Further, no smiles or winks are available, the matching engine employed is less sophisticated than those used by eHarmony and Match, and less-serious daters are part of the mix.

OUR TIME

A dating service that celebrates those 50 and over, OurTime recognizes that people in their 50s, 60s and beyond often want relationships that are quite different from what they sought in their younger years. With over 1.4 million visitors each month, this relatively-new offering doesn't just cater to those seeking a marriage relationship, but also to companionship and "something in-between." Sign-up is quick with the option to fill out each section at the onset or tackle that task later and begin searching immediately. Potential matches are generated daily and users can perform their own searches by specifying preferences. For an up-charge, members can promote their profile for greater visibility.

Pros: Profile options include photos, videos, audio and personal greetings. Live chat and a mobile application are available. Physical, electronic and procedural security measures are in place to help safeguard personal data, membership is not required to independently search for matches, send winks or see profile views by other users and the pricing model is affordable.

Cons: Limited features are available to free members, an absence of bells and whistles exists overall, and matches include those looking for casual relationships. OurTime offers a smaller dating pool than found on larger, longer-established dating sites, as well.

PLENTY OF FISH

One of the largest free dating services in the world, boasting 150 million registered users worldwide, Plenty of Fish (POF) offers its members features that include its own Chemistry Test to measure personal characteristics, a matching system that tracks user actions and tweaks suggested matches accordingly, easy navigation, fun ways to communicate with matches and an upgrade option that allows access to additional services. Signing up takes less than 30 minutes and the process is straightforward. Members complete a mix of closed and open-ended questions and fill out a personal description. Basic, advanced and geographic searches are offered.

Pros: POF is a free-to-use site with paid upgrades that offer advanced features. Instant messaging is provided, virtual gifts can be sent, varied search options are included and a mobile app is available. Its Meet Me feature allows for searches defined by a specific geographic area.

Cons: Privacy features and customer support are lacking, no live chat is offered and the dating pool includes a high percentage of less-serious daters given it's a free service.

ZOOSK

Beginning its life as a Facebook application, Zoosk employs a behavioral matchmaking engine that continually analyzes user actions to improve matches. It's currently one of the largest online dating services with over 35 million members, is both fun and accessible, and sports many beneficial features. Members are provided with scientifically-chosen matches every 24 hours and given the ability to send likes, smiles, virtual gifts and priority messages. International dating and a mobile application are also included, as is a feature that offers members the option to indicate interest levels on suggested matches. Sign-up is quick and easy, as is filling in the usual info such as age, location, education level, ethnicity and body type. Additional personal data is added over time to improve the quality of the matches provided.

Pros: Zoosk provides daily matches to members based on its behavioral engine and also allows member-initiated searches. Both free and premium members can reply to all correspondence, member profiles are updated based on site activity and ID verification is incorporated for user safety. Tools are provided for organizing and tracking communication with other members, a mobile app is offered and the service is fun to use. Invisible browsing is available for an added cost.

Cons: Zoosk lacks a personality profile, integrates with Facebook and Twitter (explained below), and allows users to register who are separated but not divorced. It's also one of the costlier services, specifically with its add-ons.

AVOID THE MEAT MARKET

So far, we've just examined online dating services, all of which offer companion mobile applications except for Chemistry. But, those aren't the only options. Many app-only alternatives exist including those mentioned above, Bumble, Coffee Meets Bagel, Happn, Hinge, Tastebuds and Tinder. Unlike the dating services, many of these mobile apps are free to use, require little set up, are photo-intensive and employ a real-time geolocation feature that makes results more immediate.

In most cases, all that's required to get started with these apps are basic bits of information that include your name, age, gender, location, short bio and a photo. Once complete, a steady stream of pictures appears showing potential matches. Connecting with others is based predominantly on looks and the majority of singles use these applications for casual meetups rather than as a means to finding long-term relationships.

Are they worth considering? In my estimation, no. More than anything else, they're "meat market" apps basing compatibility on attractiveness and initial impressions above other factors. Little effort is made to match partners based on considerations other than basic shared interests. In most cases, the data provided is too sparse to make an informed judgement. You're better off sticking with traditional online dating sites and using the apps associated with them. Remember, the purpose of this book is to assist you in finding the love of your life, not a casual fling or hook-up.

I'll go further and offer a note of caution here. Resist using any dating application, or online service for that matter, that requires you to use Facebook, Twitter or any other social media account for sign-up or verification purposes. It may make the registration process easier, but it's also likely to provide too much personal data to those who may misuse it. Honestly, you don't want to have these accounts tied to an online dating service or app. If the site you choose to employ gives the option of using your email or social media account to sign up, always select the email option and use an address created specifically for online dating. We'll cover setting up a free dating-only email account, as well as a dating-specific Google Voice phone number, in the next chapter. Both will serve you well.

CHOOSE THE RIGHT SITE

Okay, that wraps up this condensed overview of the most popular online dating services, leaving you with a decision to make. So, do your homework. Ask for recommendations from people you know and trust who have successfully found love online. Avoid the advice given by those who only have criticism to offer, as well as complaints lodged by disgruntled daters who know little about dating online, how the services operate, dealing with others in a courteous manner or how to safeguard themselves against the swindlers and players who populate all aspects of life. Read up on each service that you're considering and then make the best decision possible. Also, be advised that the individual features provided by each online dating service may change over time, some being modified or removed and others added. As such, the included summaries may not accurately reflect what's available when you read this book.[5]

Try out a site or two via free trials first and see what suits your needs best. Block out a weekend or several days to invest in the process and don't rush or spread yourself too thin. If you decide on a paid membership, my personal recommendation, look for special promotions, usually for a discounted three-month period. Again, please refer to the Online Dating Resources page at the *Discovering Love Online* website for specials being offered.

Finally, when you consider the cost of using a paid service, keep the following in mind. You can join most subscription-based offerings for approximately the same amount per month that you would spend on a moderately-priced dinner or two. It's just not that expensive. To put it another way, look at online dating as an investment in your future and not just an added expense. You need to ask yourself the simple question, "What's it worth to find the love of my life?"

At this point, you may be thinking that, like many authors, I'm only going to give you a list of online dating services, but not commit to a recommendation. Well, it always annoys me when someone else does that. So, I won't do it to you. I have family and friends who met on ChristianMingle and eHarmony, as well as acquaintances who found each other through Match and Plenty of Fish. Each site served its purpose. However, if I was asked to recommend a single service, it would be eHarmony. It's easy to use, secure and offers a great online dating experience. It's also where I met my wife, Deb.

PUT SAFETY FIRST

Your relationship should be a safe haven not a battlefield.
The world is hard enough already.

—Anonymous

I n case you had doubts, online dating carries some inherent risks. News stories relate accounts of those duped out of large sums of money through romance scams and of women, in particular, assaulted by someone they met online. I'm not trying to induce paranoia or give you the heebie-jeebies, but the threats are real and you need to be extremely careful to avoid the wrong people in your search for Mr. or Mrs. Right.

Don't assume, however, that the dangers associated with online dating are unique. They simply reflect the evils of our society. You could just as easily be in peril from an unprincipled individual you meet at a local mall, grocery store, library, fitness center, park, concert, restaurant or even your place of worship. It's unfortunate, but true. Consequently, don't let the reports you hear deter you from enjoying the rewards of online dating.

How should you respond to potential dangers? Start by keeping your wits about you and refrain from taking any unnecessary risks. Don't reveal too much personal information and watch for telltale signs of those devious sorts who want to take advantage of you—scammers, players and predators. Before we even discuss setting up your profile, I'll address these dangers and how you can guard yourself against them. Let's begin by examining how to maintain control of your personal data.

GUARD PERSONAL INFORMATION

While it should go without saying, you need to guard how much personal information you disclose in your profile and share in communication with a potential mate. Unfortunately, as in the offline world, not everyone you meet online is honest. In fact, a large percentage of online daters lie both in their profiles and in their correspondence. According to the Pew Research Center, 54 percent of online daters "have felt that someone else seriously misrepresented themselves in their profile."[1]

We're not talking about men and women who subtract a few years from their age or shave off a couple pounds of body mass, although many are guilty of these exaggerations in their profiles. I'm referring to unscrupulous characters who seek to separate you from your hard-earned money or, worse, attempt to cause you emotional and bodily harm. Sadly, purveyors of online romance scams and sexual predators abound, placing your personal and financial well-being at risk. How can you neutralize these threats and ensure your safety? By being especially cautious. Preventive safety begins with both what you choose to share and what you refrain from sharing with would-be suitors. Your motto should always be the age-old saying, "Better safe than sorry."

Accordingly, safety dictates that you keep personal information to a minimum. Use only your first name or username in your profile and early correspondence. It's unwise and unnecessary to include your surname. Although, and I'm addressing women here, you'll eventually want to know your intended's last name so you don't unknowingly set yourself up to become a Carrie Oakey, Rose Bush, Shanda Lear or something even worse should your relationship blossom.

Omit all of your other personal contact information, as well. Never share your home or work address, email address or phone number in your profile or other forms of early communication. Keep your friends' and relatives' contact info private, too. For your own safety and theirs. Don't disclose your social media presence just yet either. Not until someone has fully gained your trust. You don't want to be friends with or followed by a date gone bad or stalker, do you?

You may also want to list your city of residence as the nearest major city and not your exact town. That makes it more difficult for others to unearth your personal data and helps guard against any inappropriate activity. You should take note, as well, that some services do a much better job than others of protecting your identity and privacy.

I also recommend setting up a separate email address for your dating service profile or using the internal email system if one's available. Google's Gmail,[2] my personal recommendation, and

Yahoo Mail[3] are among the best free email services going. Using a dating-specific email address protects you against unwanted correspondence from those you choose not to communicate with regardless of your reasons. It can easily be cancelled and replaced when needed.

Another excellent idea is to set up a free Google Voice[4] account for date-related use. It redirects all incoming phone calls to your number of choice and allows you to place calls from your Google Voice account, hiding your personal number in the process. If you start receiving unwanted calls, simply block the offending number. As a benefit, your Google Voice phone service shares the same account with your dating email address, should you choose to go with Gmail, and the number can be easily rerouted if needed.

In a similar vein, if at any time in your correspondence you're harassed or receive threats from a disgruntled dater, maintain a digital paper trail. Save emails, voice messages and chat logs that contain hostile remarks so you have evidence of this behavior to provide to the dating service and authorities, if necessary.

Remember, your safety is first and foremost. Don't share any personal information until you feel entirely comfortable doing so. If someone balks at or ridicules your stance or tries to change your mind, they don't have your best interests at heart.

IGNORE FINANCIAL PLEAS

While many people legitimately seek a life partner through online dating, unscrupulous characters lurk about seeking to prey upon the innocent. You need to safeguard yourself and your children, if you have any, from them. This includes charlatans of seduction who want to bilk you out of your hard-earned financial resources. Obviously, and I hope it is obvious, don't send anyone you meet online any money...ever. Ignore their requests and report them to the online dating service immediately.

Almost 1.3 million complaints with regard to impostor scams, including romance ploys, were reported by consumers in 2016 according to the Federal Trade Commission,[5] ranking second-highest in consumer complaints that year. Furthermore, the FBI reported that Americans were cheated out of $82 million in online-dating fraud just during the last six months of 2014 as related in *Consumer Reports*,[6] a number that's low since many victims don't report the crime out of embarrassment. So, if someone you've never met in person asks you for money, you can bet they're a con artist. Cease communication immediately.

Not only are scammers out to swindle the lonely-hearted, but identity thieves want to abscond with your personal data. By gaining access to enough identifying information, a criminal can assume your identity to conduct a wide range of transactions. They can apply for bank loans and credit cards, make fraudulent withdrawals from your accounts and obtain goods and services in your name. Once this happens, it can take an indefinite amount of time to clean up the mess.

How do you avoid these miscreants? First, be wary of potential matches that include only one or two photos of an individual who looks like an Olympic athlete or movie star, usually accompanied by an incomplete written profile. Other telltale indicators include those asking to bypass the dating service's guided communication process, if it has one, or wanting to communicate via an outside email address or messaging service. Another ploy is claiming to be from the U.S. and currently traveling, living or working abroad, including deployed military personnel. References to "destiny" or "fate" bringing you together, claims of being recently widowed, requests for your address under the pretense of sending flowers or gifts, and emails containing links to questionable websites should all raise red flags.

Finally, in keeping with sound fiscal judgement, make yourself an unwavering promise to never give out financial information of any kind to someone you don't know. Keep bank information, credit card numbers and your social security number to yourself. Never divulge usernames or passwords, either. Always remain in complete control of your personal information, as well as your online dating experience. In the early stages of a relationship, anonymity is your best friend.

BEWARE EMOTIONAL PIRANHAS

Of course, safety extends beyond financial scams. Fake personas not only allow married men and women to haunt online dating sites seeking a fling or an affair, but players, too. These lowlifes toy with people's thoughts and emotions while exploiting their vulnerability to get what they want. It usually amounts to a desire to exert power over another person, put someone else down to make themselves look better, seek a sexual outlet or some other self-serving purpose. Emotional piranhas promise everything and deliver nothing except for heartache, leaving you the worse for having allowed them into your life.

So, watch carefully for clues that you may be dealing with an untrustworthy individual. In addition to the cautions I mentioned above with regard to financial safety, keep a lookout for anyone who appears more interested in themselves than you. Be wary of those who only want to email or text, but not meet face-to-face. Or conversely, anybody who wants to move immediately to an in-person rendezvous. Also, beware of those who make grandiose promises, anyone who has been active on a dating site for an extremely long period of time (possibly years) and any individual who brings up inappropriate matters or wants to discuss sex with you before you've even met for a first date.

Again, I don't mean to discourage you from seeking love via the Internet. I wouldn't have written this book if that were true. I just want to caution you and encourage you to be careful.

DODGE POTENTIAL PREDATORS

Dealing with predators is usually the first safety consideration that comes to mind for those venturing into the world of virtual dating, especially women. Unsurprisingly, according to a popular online poll, the greatest fear for women is that they'll end up dating a serial killer. Not so with the guys, regardless of whether or not they've seen the film *So, I Married an Axe Murderer*. Humorously (or sadly, depending on your viewpoint), for the majority of men their chief concern is that their date will be fat.

Regardless of your fears, physical safety is a crucial and needful concern. Always meet your potential match in a public place and stay in public. Don't ride with them in their vehicle or your own, and don't follow them back to their residence or invite them to yours. Also, make sure a friend or family member knows your plans—who you're meeting, when and where you're going and when you plan to return. Then, check in with them afterward. If you're a bit unsure about the person you're meeting, ask someone to go along with you. Arrive early and have them sit nearby so they can call you if you need to "excuse yourself" from your date.

Items containing personal information like day planners, purses and cellphones should be kept with you at all times, including short trips to the restroom. Keep your cellphone charged in case you need to use it. And, stay sober. However, if you choose to imbibe, and some of you will, keep that drink in sight to prevent tampering. That includes non-alcoholic beverages, too.

For those engaging in a long-distance relationship, a few added precautions should be observed. Stay in a hotel, not with your prospective mate. Keep the location confidential, too. Check into your room before you see each other for the first time and choose a public setting for your meeting as you would with any first date. Not the hotel bar or restaurant, but somewhere off-site.

If you can't afford a hotel, don't make the trip. Suggest that they do the traveling instead. Finally, secure your own ride. Either rent a car or use a taxi. To reiterate the above, never get into a personal vehicle with someone you've never met before.

As a general safety precaution, women should always carry a means of self-protection. At minimum, keep a pocketable defense spray such as Mace Triple Action Pepper Spray[7] in your purse or pocket (it's what I purchased for my wife and step-daughters). Taking a self-defense course is advisable, too, whether you're dating or not. Of course, many men and women are opting to carry a concealed handgun. If you decide to follow this route, please get proper training on its operation and use. In any case, don't carry a firearm unless you're prepared to use it.

Always watch for warning signs including, among other things, anyone who doesn't show up at the designated time and place, or won't provide you with a phone number to call if you end up running late or get lost. Beware of someone with an inordinate amount of spelling and grammatical errors in their profile. Don't jump to conclusions if a problem arises, but pay attention to any emerging patterns. Catching anyone in one or more lies is cause to block them and cease contact, as well as excuse yourself if you're with them in person.

Further, if you think a date is following you post rendezvous, don't try to "lose them" on the way home. It could lead to an accident. You don't want to show them where you live either. Rather, head for the nearest authorities (know the location ahead of time). You simply can't be too careful.

PERFORM DUE DILIGENCE

Some dating experts recommend hiring a private investigator to run background checks on matches. If you fall for someone big time yet have concerns about anything that just doesn't add up, it could be a worthwhile investment. However, in the initial stages of correspondence with potential life partners, I believe it's overkill. Instead, I suggest performing your own free background checks by utilizing available search tools and social media services. And, please do so before your first date.

In regard to online searches, Google[8] is your go-to tool for checking on potential matches. Of course, it works best if you can acquire a full name without giving yours away in the process. But, if the person you're corresponding with doesn't want to disclose their surname early on, you can still engage in research using other available information. Helpful data to know includes a first name, city of residence (current and past), place of birth, and their employer or the type of work they pursue. You should be able to glean most of these tidbits through your pre-date correspondence. Facebook[9] and LinkedIn[10] profiles may also provide worthwhile information if the person in question makes use of those social media services. Instagram[11] is becoming quite popular, as well.

Several other no-cost search tools are available from Intelius.[12] Options provided for performing your own simple background investigations include a basic People Search, Background Check, Criminal Records search and Reverse Phone Number Lookup. Obviously, the data Intelius provides is rudimentary, their goal being to persuade you to pay for detailed reports. Still, what you can discover for free may be worth the time invested. It certainly doesn't hurt to try.

If you elect to purchase paid reports from Intelius or a similar provider, please read the fine print carefully. Some services are subscription-based and choosing them will enroll you in their automatic renewal program. Formerly, the Better Business Bureau identified a pattern of complaints from consumers about billing issues, mostly from those unaware of ongoing monthly fees when making a one-time purchase.

Google's Reverse Image Search Tool[13] and TinEye's Reverse Image Search[14] may prove helpful, as well. Just drag and drop a profile picture into the search window on either of these web-based services and if the image appears anywhere else online you'll know momentarily. Both are valuable tools you can use to verify if your potential match's profile photo just looks like an actor or model, or if it actually belongs to one.

In all fairness, remember that I previously stated you shouldn't disclose any unnecessary personal information in the early stages of communication. That makes it rather unfair to ask someone else to share that info with you and then not disclose your own. Still, they may choose to do so freely when corresponding with you. So, take notes!

As you perform your detective work, pay attention to anything that looks suspicious and address it before you meet in person. If you receive a dubious response or have any bad feelings about a prospective match, cease communication. If anyone dodges your questions or refuses to share personal information with you at all, there's probably a reason and it's likely not good. Either they're not really committed to finding a life partner or they may be trying to hide something. If so, it's best to simply move on.

Finally, if your potential match seems to have everything going for him or her including good looks, prestige, money, expensive possessions and a long list of accolades, be wary, particularly given the above. If someone sounds too good to be true, well, you know the rest.

I can't urge you strongly enough, gals especially, to date safely. Any cause for concern that arises or gut feelings you can't shake should be taken into account. Don't give in to the fear of missing the One by moving forward with anyone you have strong doubts about. Additionally, those of faith can seek further discernment and wisdom from God. "Ask and it will be given to you,"[15] right? In the end, however, it's your call. Make it a good one.

CHAPTER FOUR

CREATE A WINNING PROFILE

Be yourself. Everyone else is already taken.

—*Oscar Wilde*[1]

When I began my initial foray into online dating, I was quite surprised by the number of matches I received with incomplete profiles. None of these biographical sketches were recently added either, and some hadn't been altered in months based on posted activity. Photographs were noteworthy by their absence, basic information fields were blank and profile questions remained unanswered. If you've stuck with me this far, you can guess my response.

Your online profile is your dating resumé. It's either going to get you an "interview" or land you in the reject pile. Don't cut corners when creating it. Among other things, you want your profile to accurately describe yourself, honestly reflect your story and paint a memorable picture that others won't forget.

MAKE A GREAT IMPRESSION

Being accurate and honest when creating your profile should be a no-brainer. Yet, for many potential suitors, it doesn't seem to register or matter. Embellishing the facts and stretching the truth are employed without a second thought. Yet, being truthful does matter. No one wants to be the target of lies, even little white ones. They always come back to bite you in the tush.

Of course, you know better, don't you? If your parents were like mine, you heard an appropriate, time-worn adage at least once in your lifetime, and most likely many times. "Honesty is the best policy."[2] Bear that in mind as your profile needs to accurately represent you—the real you. Not who you were before, not who you would like to be someday or who you wish you were already, but who you actually are today. It's the only way you're going to discover your match, the person looking for you.

In addition, your profile needs to be memorable. It's your first impression, so make it a good one. Scratch that. Make it a great one! As another age-old axiom states, "You only get one chance to make a first impression." Your profile needs to show you at your absolute best, and it must stand out amid a sea of look-a-likes. When someone comes to your profile, it should make them stop and take notice, as well as pique their interest to know more.

Before you start filling out your bio, however, you'll need to choose a profile name to use and complete any relationship questionnaire the site employs. Some sites will use your first name automatically and others will allow you to create your own. If you're given that option, you have two choices: use your first name or think of one or more words that describe you and use them to fashion your online moniker. If you choose the latter, be creative and not clichéd. Personally, I find most profile names to be either corny or contrived. I would much rather converse with a Heather, Susan, Marianne or Deb than with a BrownEyedGal, FarFromPerfect or SexyMomma. But, that's just me. Incidentally, guys can be just as guilty with their choice of online persona.

TAKE QUESTIONNAIRES SERIOUSLY

Most online dating services employ a relationship questionnaire to help match you with other singles. Completing these can take anywhere from a few minutes to an hour or longer depending on how in-depth the site is with its questions and how thorough you are with your answers. For example, eHarmony employs one of the most detailed questionnaires. It took me a little over an hour to complete (they have since condensed it). OkCupid's Dating Persona Test required just about 10 minutes, while Chemistry's preliminary assessment took a brief two minutes (it's followed up with a longer personality test once you register). I finished Match's questionnaire in about half an hour.

I urge you to take these questionnaires seriously as they offer insights into who you are, how you're perceived by others and what needs you have in a partner. Results are used to match you with those who are most compatible in your quest for the love of your life. Don't overthink your answers, but try to provide careful and truthful replies.

Relationship questionnaires can be time-consuming, but they're extremely beneficial to the matching process. So, don't just rocket through to get them out of the way.

ADJUST PREFERENCES CAREFULLY

Another matter you'll need to address is setting your personal search preferences. Each dating service is slightly different in this regard, but the choices are similar. Keep in mind that filtering selections here will affect the quality and number of compatible matches you receive. So, some adjustments may be necessary. I had to tweak my distance settings several times, reducing the search radius until I was happy with the results.

What preferences can you adjust? Usually, the options include basics such as race, religion, education, age, height, distance and factors such as your level of acceptance with regard to smoking and drinking, as well as your desires concerning children. Other settings include political affiliation, marital status, activity level, body type and willingness to relocate.

As you establish your filtering preferences, keep in mind that you can always modify them later if you find you're receiving too many matches, not enough or some that just don't conform to your criteria. You'll also find that making occasional adjustments can present you with some interesting matches to consider that you otherwise may have missed.

WRITE A COMPELLING STORY

Okay, it's time to create your profile. We'll start with the written content then proceed to the photos. But first, I'll begin with a confession. I'm a writer by vocation. I've written thousands of articles over the course of a 30-plus year profession. Experience in public speaking and teaching adorns my portfolio, as well. So, when I filled out my profile, it was nothing out of the ordinary to me, just another version of my written bio and personal story that I've jotted down, tweaked, appended and shared on numerous occasions in the past. For most of you, however, coming up with a solid, engaging profile is going to be real work. In fact, talking about yourself may not come naturally at all. Don't fret. That's what this chapter's all about.

When creating content for your personal bio and composing responses to predefined questions, be creative and include a hook to draw people into your story. You want to catch their attention and pique their interest. Steer clear of clichéd starters such as, "Hi, my name's Brett and I like to watch movies, eat out and go hiking." Instead, begin with something interesting and original like, "Hey, I'm Brianna, but my friends call me Bri! I'm always up for a great evening of fine dining, but I also love peanut butter sandwiches! How about you?" Don't just state facts, but tell an engaging story. It will result in a greater number of profile views, and that's what you want.

Overall, be positive about yourself and others. Portray an optimistic outlook on life. Make sure that you list your positive qualities, giftedness and what you can bring to a relationship, not just what you're looking for in someone else. You want others to know you're a good catch, but without putting it in those exact words. Again, use a story format to show potential partners who you are, don't just tell them.

When completing the written parts of your profile, please apply proper grammar, spelling and punctuation. Use a word processor if necessary and copy your finished work to your profile when it's ready. Exhibit the correct use of upper and lowercase letters, too. SHOUTING is a violation of netiquette. Don't abbreviate either.

Acronyms such as "lol" and "l8r" make you look lazy at best. You want Mr. or Mrs. Right to know you're educated and normal.

ANSWER QUESTIONS ACCURATELY

Beyond a personal bio, each dating service is different in the amount and type of written content they allow. Some are very open-ended while others ask you to respond to statements like "The most important thing I'm looking for in a person is...," "I typically spend my leisure time..." and "The three things that I'm most thankful for are...." It's in your best interest to not leave any of these blank and to be original in your responses.

To illustrate, don't complete a statement such as "The first thing people notice about me..." with a brief and overused "is my smile" or something equally boring and unoriginal. Rather, be engaging and noteworthy. Elaborate with a response like, "my smile, boyish good looks and charm. Actually, that's three things, isn't it?" In doing so, you'll distinguish yourself from other matches. Such an answer shows that you're thoughtful and creative, and that you do indeed have a sense of humor.

Do you also possess and own up to any geek tendencies? Toss in a reference that conveys it. Love *Star Trek* and *Doctor Who*? Say so. Enjoy baking and scrapbooking? Share that, too. Maybe you have some interesting hobbies such as birdwatching, astronomy, lapidary arts,[3] juggling or model railroading. If so, acknowledge them. Whatever sets you apart from the great unmarried masses helps make you more attractive to your future mate, within reason and apart from any overtly strange quirks. In other words, it's best to keep certain things under wraps until later in your relationship such as your imported garden gnomes, taxidermied jackalopes or monogrammed underwear.

When you answer your profile questions, be as specific as possible and avoid trite remarks. You may enjoy walking on the beach, watching sunsets and hanging with your friends, but who doesn't? Be honest with your answers, but let your humor shine through and keep your responses succinct. With regard to humor, use amusing lines or quotes to spice up your profile. It will make prospective matches smile and maybe even laugh. As a side note, in case you didn't know, laughing increases dopamine in the brain, the "feel good" neurotransmitter that helps to regulate emotional responses. Consequently, a good peppering of humor may help you win over a prospective match. It's not being manipulative as long as it's the real you being portrayed.

One thing to keep in mind regarding your profile is that it's designed to give others a glimpse of yourself, not a complete history. If your written content is too long, others are likely to give up and look elsewhere. So, resist the temptation to elaborate. You can delve into the details in your one-on-one correspondence and on dates. For now, simply create curiosity and interest. Think of your profile as the appetizer. The entrée and dessert come later.

DISCLOSE IMPORTANT DETAILS

What information should appear in your profile? I suggest that you share short, interesting stories and experiences that allow others to acquire a glimpse into who you are and what motivates you. Communicate likes and dislikes, hobbies and interests, personal qualities, passions and goals. Again, include what you're seeking in a lifetime partner, along with what you have to offer someone else. Also endeavor to make your profile engaging so your soon-to-be love interest can't wait to know more about you.

Furthermore, people usually tend to remember the first and last things someone shares with them. So, make sure those bits of your profile truly stand out, displaying confidence, charm, creativity, warmth and other positive qualities. Go beyond what's required and you're sure to stand apart from the crowd.

You should include whether or not you have or want children, as well. If you still have any living at home, you need to disclose that information now rather than springing it on someone later. Otherwise, it will reflect negatively.

Moreover, if you're the parent of a special needs child, it's extremely important for you to be honest about that fact up front. Unfortunately, for many this will be a deal-breaker. So, be careful how you phrase the matter. In such cases, I believe you need to include this information in your profile. It's much better to rule out anyone at the start who won't be accepting of the situation than go through one rejection after another once they find out. Just be as positive about it as you can. Details aren't necessary at this point. A simple statement like, "I have a special needs child who I hope you'll grow to love as much as I do" is enough. If you're not truthful, your prospective partner will feel deceived when they find out. I'll also mention in this regard that you need to be willing to accept someone else with their special needs child, too. It works both ways.

Along the same lines, if you have any deal-breakers of your own—pets, sports, the great outdoors, smoking, drinking—clarify those up front. It makes no sense to consider dating someone if non-negotiables are on the table from the start, no matter how close that person is to your ideal in other respects.

Are you a person of faith? If so, you need to make that clear. If you and your partner aren't on the same page spiritually, you can anticipate major conflicts to arise sooner or later. It's best to make your faith explicit from the start and avoid having to face a difficult choice later on between your intended and God. Fail in this regard and every aspect of your relationship will be negatively affected.

KNOW WHAT TO EXCLUDE

It's also imperative to exclude certain things from your profile. Omit negative tones, comments and demands, and don't belittle yourself or rag on a previous spouse or steady. For example, if you lack a fondness for cats, don't write "I hate cats." Instead, employ a positive statement like "I'm looking for someone who loves dogs." Was your previous spouse a real piece of work? Steer clear of saying "I'm looking for a partner who's not a jerk." How about a congenial, "I'm ready to meet a kind and loving person." Always choose affirmative phrasing. It makes all the difference in how you're perceived by others.

Please refrain from sharing your dating horror stories, as well. Nothing good will come from complaining about all the losers or weirdos you've gone out with in the past. All it will accomplish is to convey that you're apparently a poor judge of character, and that you make repeated mistakes in whom you choose to date.

Oh, and don't look or act desperate in your profile or in your correspondence. You're likely to attract predators and turn away possible suitors if you do.

CHOOSE PHOTOS WISELY

Being accurate, honest and memorable relates to your photos, too. Although pictures don't communicate the entire story, they're integral in creating a great first impression. Choose them wisely. You only have a fraction of time to capture someone's attention visually, about 40 milliseconds according to a study conducted by the periodical *Psychological Science*.[4] That's how quick most people are when it comes to drawing conclusions regarding the subject in a photo. A poorly selected image, an old one or none at all is the quickest way to lose a potential love interest before they even have a chance to read the written profile you worked so hard to craft.

Typically, I recommend avoiding selfies, even if you're tempted to use them. More often than not they distort your appearance and present you in an unflattering light. Although, I do admit that they seem to hold greater appeal among younger daters. If you fall into that demographic, feel free to experiment. Otherwise, my original recommendation stands.

Also, stay away from old, out-of-date pictures. No 10-years-old or 20-pounds-lighter photos. I'm being gracious here given the antiquity of the images some folks post. They're nothing short of outright deception. Using them will have negative repercussions, so stick with photographs that are less than a year old, and taken specifically for your online bio if possible. Again, think of your profile as a resumé and incorporate your best shots.

Don't include pets in your photos either, at least not in your main image. If you simply must, keep it to one shot and make sure you're in the picture with them. I don't share this as a matter of personal preference, but based on supporting data. According to a survey conducted by Zoosk,[5] main profile photos featuring pets receive as much as 53 percent fewer responses than those without, so don't limit yourself unnecessarily.

I'll be honest with you in this regard. I shamelessly blocked several women whose main profile photos showed them with their arms wrapped around their big, slobbery dogs. Sorry, I don't hate pooches, but I'm also not a fan of the canine crowd, nor do I want to compete with them in any way (cats are a different story). I also blocked one woman who chose to use a picture of a guinea pig for her main profile image. She wasn't even in the picture, just the furry little varmint. Equally lame, it was the only snapshot she chose to include in her profile.

Was that the most tactful way of dealing with these women? Maybe not on some sites, but on eHarmony (remember, that's where my wife and I met) it's actually okay. When you block someone on this service, they receive a message that you have moved on so it's not shown as a rejection. If, however, someone contacts you and you're not inclined to correspond with them, reply kindly and say something like, "Thanks for writing, but I'm not interested." I suggest you avoid giving reasons why. It's not necessary and usually adds hurt to any feelings of rejection that already exist.

I encountered other photo faux pas along the way, as well. Many of the matches I received featured main profile images that consisted of high school or college graduation photos, sideways pictures, blurry images, big scary grins, blank expressions, photos of guys (remember, these were profiles of women) and one of Lucille Ball. If a picture is really worth a thousand words, make sure the words you're sending are the right ones.

PAINT AN ACCURATE PICTURE

Quality photos are crucial to your profile, so invest in some new photographs taken by a friend, family member or professional photographer (but not studio shots). Lifestyle photos work best, taken in several locations and wearing a few different outfits if you can swing it. Choose the locale carefully as it says a lot about you. Beach or bar? Coffee shop or concert hall? Park bench or Park Avenue? It does make a difference. Include at least one head shot and one full-body image, with additional photos preferred. Between five and eight would be good. Just make sure they portray you accurately, and doing the things you enjoy. In other words, show the potential love of your life what he or she can expect.

Select a sharply-focused head-and-shoulders (bust) or head-to-waist (torso) shot for your primary photo, preferably the first. A face-only close-up or full-body image can negatively affect how people perceive you according to the blog at *Photofeeler*,[6] an online photo testing tool. With regard to likability, for the former, as well as competence and influence, for the latter.

Of these two midrange poses, head-and-shoulders pics give folks a better glimpse of your face and offer increased visibility on dating services that employ small thumbnails to provide a quick view of available matches. If you choose a head-to-waist or full-body shot for your main photo, your face will be unrecognizable when reduced in size. You're simply asking to be overlooked. If people can't see what you look like, they'll be less likely to click on your profile. So, stick with a head-and-shoulders pose.

Steer clear of group photos. You don't want any competition for your attention, nor do you want someone contacting you to ask about your friend or sibling. Furthermore, don't use snapshots with your ex cut out, showing an arm around your shoulder or waist. That's tacky and gives off bad vibes.

Likewise, nix pictures with sunglasses. People want to view your eyes, not a reflection. Smile and make eye contact. A serious look can be beneficial, too, as long as it's not the only image you use. Some women prefer seeing a man glance away from the camera as it adds a sense of mystery, but smiling and looking directly at the camera worked for me as it has for many others.

Shun photos that show too much skin. They'll attract the wrong people, players rather than soulmates. Don't be too businesslike in your photos either. Convey a relaxed and fun tone unless that's just not you. Be aware of what's in the background, as well. You don't want any embarrassing surprises (a great reason to avoid selfies and mirror shots, especially in the bathroom).

On a more controversial note, some dating experts recommend that you avoid posting photos of your children for safety reasons. I understand their concern. However, if you handle it correctly and don't share any detailed personal information about them, I believe it's okay to include one current photo with you and your kids. They're a part of the whole package and will help endear you to the right potential suitors while eliminating others. Not having offspring of my own, I was looking for someone with older children. Thus, for me, it was a bonus to see a photograph of my future wife and her two teenage daughters.

Additionally, bear in mind that others will pick up signals and make assumptions based on your photos. So, strive to look your best and make an excellent first impression. Portray a calm and confident persona, smile and act natural. Don't hide anything by doctoring your photos. If you're not the person someone's seeking, it's better to be turned down online rather than face-to-face.

For those inclined to take their own photos and have a friend or family member serve as a photographer, posing guides are available to assist. You'll find links to several on the Online Dating Resources page at *Discovering Love Online*. By the way, when you've completed your profile, I strongly recommend asking a friend or family member to look it over. You don't want to have any cringeworthy typos or inappropriate content detracting from the finished product.

So, there you go! These tips should help you weave together an accurate and winsome profile. Just make sure it truly represents you. Your goal should be to receive a response like I did from my then wife-to-be. When we met in person for the first time, she remarked, "You look like you stepped right out of your profile."

Remember. You're seeking the love of your life, and you want to find someone who loves you for who you are today.

CHAPTER FIVE

FIND THE BEST MATCHES

You can't evaluate a prospective partner if you insulate your relationship from your family and friends—and his [or hers].

—*Harriet Lerner*

By the time you've completed your personal inventory, gained insight into what makes you tick, selected the dating site you plan to use and wrapped up your profile, you'll have invested significant time and energy. Thankfully, this is where the payoff begins. It's now time to evaluate the matches sent your way or those you've handpicked, depending on the matching features offered by the dating service you chose.

Hopefully, the matches you receive will include those who have invested efforts on par with your own in their quest for the love of a lifetime. Realistically, though, you'll probably end up with a wide gamut of prospects, some who have put forth an equivalent effort to yours, a few who have exceeded your achievements and others who clearly entered the online dating arena with as much preparation as ordering a pizza. Regardless, do yourself a favor as you peruse your matches and actually read what they've written. Don't just skim profiles. The only way you'll know if you've found a potential life partner is to be diligent at this stage.

PREPARE TO MEET YOUR MATCH

Eliminating poor matches is an important and necessary aspect of the online dating process. However, keeping them from landing in your "inbox" in the first place is preferable. What's the best way to ensure that you only receive quality results? Start, as discussed previously, by creating a stellar profile. That's step one. Step two involves thoughtfully completing the dating service's relationship questionnaire, accurately setting your demographic preferences and ensuring you're clear and concise in your profile regarding who you are, as well as what you're seeking and what you wish to avoid in a relationship.

A word to the wise, don't take a service's match suggestions too seriously, but with a grain of salt. They're just recommendations based on the data you've supplied and the site's inborn matching algorithms. The potential matches offered to you could be highly accurate, barely qualified or anywhere in between. That's what I experienced when I was actively dating online and when I did my research for this book. Some sites were dead-on with the matches they provided while others were all over the board. You may discover that your own searches, on sites that permit it, prove to be more accurate. Nevertheless, your results will depend on how exact you were when you set your original profile preferences and on how capable you are of performing an accurate and detailed search by yourself.

When a prospective match first contacts you, only reply to those who show evidence that they've actually read your profile. Unless, they simply don't interest you. "Hey!" or "Want to chat?" doesn't cut it. That's a clear sign of laziness, and I certainly hope you're not willing to accept a relationship with someone who's lazy. Only reply to those who have taken time to read your profile and mention something from it or ask you a question based on it. Some sites guide you through a step-by-step process of getting to know a prospective match that helps eliminate a lot of dating spam. If your service does, take advantage of it.

Of course, always listen to your gut. If something just feels off, you're probably right. Cease corresponding or, if you haven't begun yet, don't reply or kindly decline.

BEGIN THE ELIMINATION ROUND

Unless someone stands out as an ideal match upon first glance, I suggest beginning with an elimination round. Weeding out poor matches removes distractions, allowing you to focus on the best potential companions.

Some matches can be nixed quickly and easily. Those that are clearly outside the parameters you've set fall into this category. Anyone who's significantly too old or too young won't be a fit, as are those you obviously have no physical attraction toward (just don't make a snap judgement based solely on an unflattering photo). Neither are matches who don't want kids if you still have any at home or those with children if that's not your preference.

Major differences in lifestyle and faith are particularly important considerations, too. The same with any non-negotiables that you established earlier. Don't compromise in this area. They're non-negotiable for a reason.

Blatant red flags allow you to eradicate others. Not posting a photo, only including a blurry one or showing too much skin are all negative indicators. The same holds true for profiles with very little written content or, the opposite, excessive verbiage. Anyone fresh out of a relationship or still in one, those who show signs of addictive behaviors and anybody who references sex in any way should be avoided or blocked. If anything in someone's profile gives you a sense of foreboding, move on in your search.

It's also important to gain an overall impression of what someone is like based on their profile. This, I'll caution you, can be tricky and involves some reading between the lines. Still, it's a helpful approach to employ. Do they seem to be well-adjusted, positive and reasonable? Do they convey a friendly and inviting spirit? Or, do they come across as arrogant, boastful, insincere, judgmental or bitter? If you detect any of the latter, ferret out those profiles. Also give a wide berth to anyone who appears to possess a serious lack of self-confidence and is self-debasing or unclear about what they want from life or in a relationship. Avoid people, as well, who lack direction or purpose and anybody who seems overly-needy or excessively-controlling, along with those who openly contradict themselves in their profile.

Some matches are a tougher call. If a potential companion lives too far away and you're not interested in long-distance romances, you may need to pass for now. If you don't nix them entirely, at least move them to the bottom of your list in case you want to reconsider them at a later time.

Pets may be another concern. If a possible match has a pet you're allergic to or you simply find objectionable, you can either pass or, if the match seems great in every other respect, you may want to pursue a relationship but ask early on whether the pet's future is negotiable. Some may be willing to find a new home for Fifi or Mittens in preference to gaining you in their place. But, you should know this ahead of time or it may put you in the dog house instead of Fido.

AVOID BEING NARROW-MINDED

I do want to add one caution when it comes to excluding profiles and the people attached to them. Resist being overly-picky or too restrictive. While you want to find the best match, you don't want to miss him or her because you made your criteria too narrow.

For example, ladies, don't miss out on a great guy because he's only 5' 11" and you set your filtering to 6' and taller, or because he's 52 years old and you set your search to only find guys 40-50. Same for the men out there. You could unknowingly pass on a terrific gal who's 38 years old and lives 30 miles away because you're only looking for women 35 and younger within a 25-mile radius. Don't eliminate anyone who could be an excellent match and companion by holding too closely to an ideal.

If we're being honest, the tendency most people have when dating online is to be far pickier than they ever were when dating traditionally. It's an easy trap to fall into owing to the comparative nature of a match-driven process and the ease at which someone can simply be passed over or ignored based on their profile. So, be fastidious about the important things, but let the rest go.

Unfortunately, not everyone is a talented writer or skilled at expressing themselves, so try and look past some of the profile faux pas you encounter. Yes, it's good to avoid clichés and popular phrases such as "I'm looking for true love" and "I love long walks on the beach." Nevertheless, don't flippantly discount someone who spreads them throughout their profile like butter on bread.

Equally, don't make assumptions and delete or block a match too quickly. You may just need more information about them. If so, ask. Give someone the benefit of the doubt. You can always purge them later. But, if and when you do, be kind. Let them know nicely that you're simply not a fit. You're not only dealing with profiles. You're corresponding with real people. So, treat others with the same courtesy you expect from them.

FIND THE CRÈME DE LA CRÈME

Now that the elimination round is complete, go through the rest of your potential matches with an eye toward detecting the cream of the crop. You may find it easiest to maintain a written list of your potential keepers to pursue further, placing an asterisk next to those who look the most promising. If the service you're on has a favorites feature, use it to tag them and continue through the list.

Once you've completed your first pass, read through the bios of your top choices thoughtfully. Leaf through the photos they posted and see how they answered profile questions to determine if the basis for a good match exists. Don't chintz on your time investment at this point. Be thorough. If someone appears to be a good-to-great catch, it's time to connect with them and begin the introduction process.

Also, recognize that while you're going through matches others are, too. Thus, you're likely to be contacted by interested parties while you're in the process of deciding who you want to pursue. Apply the above guidelines here, as well, and determine if you wish to connect with them or not. Just remember to be gracious whatever you decide.

KNOW WHEN LESS IS MORE

A prevailing line of thought exists among the community of dating consultants that you should correspond with and date numerous matches concurrently. Personally, I believe that's a mistake. Just because an action is possible doesn't mean it's advisable. While you may excel at balancing your budget and juggling multiple tasks simultaneously, I don't recommend that you try and juggle or balance too many matches at one time. Not only can it become confusing, but it can be quite time-consuming and expensive. Of course, it's possible you could be among the fortunate few who connect with their soulmate immediately, avoiding the need to correspond with an innumerable number of prospects. But, that's not the experience of most seeking love online.

Therefore, when it comes to determining how many matches to correspond with and date at the same time, I suggest you adopt the mantra "less is more." Start small with your short list of the most promising matches you made earlier. Correspond with two or three at a time, a half dozen at the most. Honestly, it's difficult for the majority of online daters to juggle a greater number and keep them all straight, especially if managing profiles on several dating sites. Follow this prescription and you'll increase your focus and reduce your stress levels.

If you don't hear in a day or two from the matches you contacted, or if they turned out to be duds, proceed to the next few that you selected. When further matches surface, prioritize them, adding the best to your short list. It's unlikely you'll run out of options. Still, on sites that do the matching for you, a time may come when the supply of matches begins to dwindle. Once that occurs, you can catch up on the backlog or, if necessary, broaden your search criteria to include additional prospects.

Having said that, if the addition of daily matches overwhelms you at any time, stressing you out and making it difficult to focus, temporarily hide your profile or turn off the send matches feature. It will reduce distractions and un-frazzle your nerves while you sort through the potential companions already on hand.

That's a sound bit of advice I wish I'd been given before I started dating online. Although I had spoken with several friends about their experiences, I wasn't quite ready for what I encountered "in the wild." On my first day, I was smiled at, emailed from and even asked to go directly to a phone call by enough overly-eager women that my first inclination was to block them all. I felt like the proverbial deer caught in the headlights. (Sadly, I hit one of those poor beasts recently. A deer that is, not one of the above women.) Then, over the next few days, I was bombarded by dozens of additional matches to sift through. I just wish I had realized at the time that I could have temporarily suspended further matches until I was ready.

You can only spread yourself so thin with the preponderance of responsibilities and commitments life entails, and that includes relationships. Finding the love of your life is an important task that shouldn't be rushed. You're not buying shoes, trying out a new hairstyle or purchasing a refrigerator, all of which you can easily return, change or replace if you make a mistake. You're seeking a life partner. Abbreviated correspondence and jack-rabbit dating may cause you to dismiss someone too quickly. Conversely, don't drag things out unnecessarily, but take your time and give each potential relationship sufficient consideration.

One final caveat. Be proactive and try not to allow yourself to become emotionally attached to anyone based on their profile alone, a subject I'll elaborate on later. That's like buying a car exclusively on the merits of a commercial. Things like behavior, demeanor, character and social skills are only fully disclosed in person. Do they smile frequently and make eye contact? Are they attentive or are they always checking their cellphone or watch? You won't discover this information until you're sitting across a table from someone.

CHAPTER SIX

IMPROVE COMMUNICATION SKILLS

Men and women may speak the same language, but we interpret words differently.

— *Pamela Cummins*

Online dating offers an excellent opportunity to become acquainted with someone before actually going on a date with them. Still, it's possible to invest too much time and effort communicating, mostly emailing and messaging, from behind the confines of an online service. Even beyond the point when a face-to-face meeting is prudent. Truthfully, you just won't know if a genuine attraction exists between you and your potential companion until you meet in person. Only then will you know if they possess that intangible je ne sais quoi.[1]

Nevertheless, don't abbreviate the process. An opinion held by many online dating experts is to keep correspondence brief, make a phone call and get to that all-important first date as quickly as possible. I believe that form of extremism shortchanges one of the key benefits of online dating—getting acquainted with someone well enough in advance to determine if a date is even warranted. While it's important to move things along to that initial meeting, finding the love of your life is not akin to speed dating or even casual dating. You're seeking a life partner, so aim for a balanced approach. Take advantage of the various ways to connect with and learn about someone that most online dating services offer.

SEND WINKS AND SMILES

Not all online dating services are created equal in the area of communication. Some offer multiple avenues to indicate interest, connect with and get to know a possible match before the emails commence. Others, not so much. Regardless, take advantage of the tools offered by the service you choose and reach out to those who interest you. Give smiles and winks, like photos, send ecards and virtual gifts, ask questions and take polls all before emailing or chatting. These features are great for breaking the ice and even illuminating some non-negotiables up front.

Besides being an excellent way to initiate the communication process, these flirtatious gestures and personal polls make it easy for those who are introverted to get things started. Which reminds me. Gals, you need to move past the old-fashioned convention that says you have to wait for the man to make the first move. It's entirely appropriate, and highly recommended, that you make your interest known. In a study conducted by OkCupid, it was discovered that "women are two-and-a-half times more likely to get a response than men if they initiate" the first contact.[2] That's an incredible advantage.

I will mention that while I'm quite the technology enthusiast, familiar with all forms of digital communication and competent in social skills, I approached my introduction to Internet dating with a certain degree of trepidation. Receiving smiles from several women provided the confidence to return the gesture and take the next step.

As you begin corresponding with others, don't shortchange the early stages of communication. Some over-eager prospects will desire to bypass these steps and proceed immediately to email, chat or phone calls. Resist the temptation. These tools are designed to guide you through the process of getting to know someone before investing substantial time, energy and emotion in prolonged interaction with them.

They also allow you to weed out undesirable matches. It's much wiser to earmark an hour or two for staging your way through correspondence with two or three matches than spend that time emailing or chatting with just one person. Further, those who want to speed up the process come across as either too eager, needy or with suspicious intent.

HOLD OFF ON THE CALLS

Once you've broken the ice and made it past your initial contact, move forward with email, instant messaging and chat to deepen your knowledge of potential matches. Hold off on phone calls at this point to allow time to determine if you really want to pursue this more personal form of communication. Ditto for Skype and FaceTime. In fact, a phone call prior to a first date is not necessary and could even have negative repercussions. I'll explain.

Written communication can cover a multitude of sins. It gives you time to think before asking a question or responding to one. It also hides any nervousness you may experience when talking with someone you barely know. Plus, if you have any vocal quirks such as regional accents, stuttering and stammering or distracting pauses, they won't show up in textual conversations. Not so with vocal communication.

Good or bad, it's possible you, or your prospective partner, could make a relationship decision based upon how the other sounds on the phone. If their voice reminds you of James Earl Jones or Kathleen Turner, will that be a deciding factor? What if they sound more like Pee-wee Herman or a "whiny" valley girl? Personally, I'd rather not let someone's voice, lack of phone skills or vocal characteristics color my decision on whether to meet in person or not.

Nonetheless, I do think that it's a good idea to exchange phone numbers a day or two before your first date just in case you need to reschedule or call to say you're running late. But, don't give out your personal one. Instead, provide the Google Voice number you established for this purpose.

COMMUNICATE WITH INTENTION

When dating online, your goal in corresponding with any given match is to decide if the potential exists for a lifelong relationship. This process of communication assumes many forms including email, texting, chatting, quizzes, questions, lists and flirtatious gestures like winks and smiles. While all assist in gaining insight into a prospective companion and learning what makes them tick, the bulk of your interactions will occur through email and text messaging. Consequently, you may want to polish up your written communication skills and possibly learn some new ones.

Your dialogue with others should be clear, deliberate and well written. That's a given, yet it doesn't end there. It's also important that you're able to interpret the messages you receive and not just peruse their content. As before, you need to read between the lines, if you will, taking note of what was written and also what was omitted. At the very least, it will help you formulate questions to ask in your next communication.

When corresponding with others, exhibit outstanding etiquette, being gracious and genuine. Grammar, punctuation and spelling count, too, if you want to prompt a favorable perception. I've said it before, but I'll repeat myself. First impressions are critical.

Initial emails should be kept relatively short; several paragraphs are sufficient. Resist using generic messages. Instead, be original with each person you contact. Include a brief introduction and find a point of interest to incorporate into your text—something unusual or fascinating, similar professions, or interests you have in common. Finding a topic to comment on should be easy. While you're at it, come up with a creative subject line. It should grab attention and entice others to see what you've written. It will also tell them that you actually read their profile. Some examples? "Wow! I love rappelling, too." "Yum! Italian food is my favorite!" Or, "I'm also a cat fancier. Whiskers is so cute."

In round two of your correspondence, assuming you received a response to your first message, a question or two is appropriate. You may want to ask about a concern that's important to you, get clarification on what was shared in someone's profile or inquire regarding the type of relationship being sought if that wasn't made clear. No sense getting involved with someone who's only seeking a casual arrangement when you're looking for the One.

If someone else contacts you first and their email is vague, like it could be written to anyone, pin them down to see if they really read your profile. Ask them pointed questions such as, "What in my profile interested you the most?" or "Why did you choose to write to me?" This will help eliminate those who mass-message dozens of potential matches hoping someone will respond.

By the way, don't delay more than a day or two when replying to someone. While you may be having an extremely busy week, they could perceive your silence as a lack of interest. A short text or email explaining the delay with a promise to reply soon is preferable. Even if you're not interested, be courteous and send a response such as, "Thanks, but I don't think we're a match."

For those so inclined, you can save yourself some time by creating several brief notes in advance and using the appropriate reply when needed. A text-expansion application like Breevy,[3] TextExpander[4] or Typinator[5] makes this quick and easy. Write up the note you want to send and assign an abbreviation to it. Then, type that short bit of text the next time you wish to insert your message. As an example, the above "Thanks, but I don't think we're a match" reply could be inserted by typing the shortened text "nomatch" or something similar. It's quite a time saver. I use a text expansion app every day for text replacement, to correct common typing errors and to speed up the writing process at large for emails, online posts, articles and books.

Continuing where we left off, while it's not good to delay too long in sending a reply, you don't want to respond too quickly either. It could appear that you're overly eager, desperate or don't have much of a life. So, allow between several hours and a day before replying. A little suspense is a good thing.

For most, conversations prior to a first date will be limited to non-threatening chitchat about work, hobbies and family, leaving intimate discussions until meeting in person. That said, weighty conversations are okay. How deep your discussions go prior to a first face-to-face encounter really depends on how comfortable you are putting yourself out there with relative strangers.

Some people will feel at ease conversing on just about any topic before meeting together. Others will find it too threatening to go beyond the basics. Even so, the rule of thumb is to only discuss what you're comfortable sharing and to not disclose too much early in a relationship. Dialogue involving sexual concerns and marriage are best reserved for later, after you've met in person and when it seems appropriate.

On a final note, if at any time during your correspondence you have questions about someone you're conversing with regarding what they've shared or failed to share, or if you just have a gut feeling that something is off, ask your friends and family for their thoughts. It never hurts to have a second opinion if you have any doubts or concerns.

ARRANGE A FACE-TO-FACE

At some point in your dialogue you need to ask yourself, "Is it time to meet in person?" Honestly, timing is an individual matter. When you've learned enough about someone to know you're a good match, don't procrastinate. Arrange your first date. Men, ask her out. Women, if he's not asking, suggest a meeting. A first date may be appropriate within a few days for some, while it could take longer for others. However, if you've been corresponding practically every day for several weeks, like Kip and Lafawnduh in the comedy film *Napoleon Dynamite*, you're overdue to meet in person and discover if chemistry exists.

When my wife, Deb, and I embarked on our romance, we took advantage of eHarmony's built-in communication tools to learn about each other before transitioning to the service's internal email system by answering several pre-selected Quick Questions, completing the Makes or Breaks list and then asking our own personalized Dig Deeper queries. We valued those early steps in the correspondence process.

Once the emails began, we started off slowly, posing general queries based on the content we included in our profiles, answers generated through the site's communication tools and the long list of pre-defined Q&A questions we had each answered. Around the two-week mark, we started discussing more personal matters, corresponding every other day. Then, roughly three-and-a-half weeks after our first email, we set the date to meet in person. At that point, we had learned enough about each other to know we wanted to pursue a relationship. All that remained was to see if that "spark" existed and it did.

LEARN TO SAY "NOT INTERESTED"

Unfortunately, while no one likes being rebuffed, the time will come when you'll be on the receiving end of rejection. Everyone experiences it, myself included. On the flip side, you'll likely need to tell someone else that you're not interested at some point, too. Several Internet-appropriate ways exist to do so.

If you've only received one email from someone you have no interest in pursuing, you can ignore their message and delete it. A reply, while considerate, is not required. It really depends on how personal of a message they sent you. On sites that let others know when you read or delete their emails, you can elect to reply with a brief, "Thank you for writing, but I'm not interested." If they continue to message you, don't answer. Block their emails and report them to the online dating service if necessary.

What you shouldn't do is be discourteous. When someone takes the time to write, at least open their message and read it. Deleting unopened email is rude. Don't offer a thoughtless reply either. If you choose to respond, be brief but kind.

If you're beyond a first email, or in the midst of a chat or instant message exchange, and decide the other person isn't a match, say so. End your dialogue with a statement like, "While I've enjoyed our conversation, I need to wrap it up. I don't think we're a match, but I hope you find success in your search." If they're accepting, that's great. If not, don't perpetuate an argument or a debate. Say goodbye and close the chat or instant message window. If you've been communicating via email, simply don't reply. Again, block them if necessary. You never want to be rude to anyone, but you do need to be firm.

What about phone calls? As stated previously, I suggest holding off until you've met in person. Still, if you do end up phoning first, have an exit strategy prepared in advance.

If during a phone call you decide you have no plans for the relationship to go any further, you have several options. You can tell the truth and let the other person know you have no interest. Thank them for their time and wish them well. Or, you can find a way to end the conversation without making any commitments. Then, follow up with an email to graciously let them know you're not a match and you don't see the relationship going any further. Whatever you do, don't end the conversation in a way that could lead the other person to believe you have a desire to continue communicating. Don't hang up on them either, as they may think you were cut off. Make your intent clear.

In spite of your best efforts, some people won't take "No" for an answer. Even though you're explicit in your decision to cease communicating, they'll continue to contact you. It may well be that they're clueless, desperate or have built a fantasy relationship in their mind. What should you do? As indicated above, maintain control and be firm. Don't argue, just state the facts. If they persist, inform them that unless they cease you'll report their activities as abuse to the dating service. Then, follow through and notify the powers that be about them if they decide to contact you again. Make no further replies. Delete messages unopened, unless threats necessitate keeping a "paper trail," and don't accept chats or calls. If you can block them, do so.

Hopefully, the majority of your interactions with others seeking love will be positive regardless of the form they take. That was my experience. Even so, while getting to know someone new should be exciting and rewarding, whether or not it ends in a lifelong relationship, it doesn't always work out that way.

CHAPTER SEVEN

PRACTICE FIRST-DATE ETIQUETTE

To learn etiquette, is actually learning how to see others, and respect them.

— *Yixing Zhang*

Hopefully, your efforts to date (pun intended) have brought positive results. You like what you've seen in someone's profile, their answers to your questions haven't exposed any deal-breakers, you have common values and interests, similar likes and dislikes, and you feel a level of attraction. You're ready to meet in person. Now what?

First, I advise you to consider several pre-date questions. Where and when will you meet? How should you greet each other? Are there any do's and don'ts to ponder before you arrive? What will you wear? What topics are open to discussion and which ones should you avoid? And, how will the rendezvous end? Do yourself, and your date, a favor. Think through the answers ahead of time.

COMBAT PRE-DATE JITTERS

Before we get into specifics, let me offer a bit of advice to help you prepare for your initial meeting and alleviate pre-date jitters. First, while it goes without saying, some folks need to hear it anyway. Arrive on time or a few minutes early. Showing up late without a really good reason tells your date that he or she isn't that important, a perception you don't want to convey. Moreover, it's just basic courtesy to appear on time. Remember, those first impressions matter. It's better to arrive too early, and wait nearby if necessary, than to straggle in late.

How should you act on a first date? Simple. As quoted earlier, be yourself. It's easier than trying to be someone else. Seeking to impress your date by being a phony always backfires. Your desire should be to find someone who wants you for you. For that to happen, the real you needs to be center stage. Smile, make eye contact and allow your humor to show. Also, leave your stink-face at home, unless that's the real you. It's only fair that others know what they're getting.

Honest, authentic conversation is a priority. Divulging your deepest, darkest secrets isn't required, but truthfulness is a must. You should expect the same in return. Being relaxed and not overly emotional or dramatic is important, too. We already have plenty of drama in our lives. This will help put your date at ease and encourage them to act likewise.

Being considerate and polite is also required. One of the easiest ways to kill a first date, as well as a fledgling relationship, is by being impolite and rude. No one wants to be around a thoughtless jerk, let alone marry one.

Open mindedness about your date is another important factor. If they're not quite what you expected, don't be too quick to write them off. Some people are nervous and self-conscious when they meet someone new. Others may be extra talkative in an effort to hide first-date butterflies. It may just take a little effort on your part to put them at ease, allowing the real person to shine through.

Don't do anything that makes you feel uncomfortable either. If your date's behavior or conversation is inappropriate, let them know. Should they continue, excuse yourself and leave. If they act that way the first time you meet, know for a fact it will only worsen with time. It's best to part ways now.

KEEP DATES AFFORDABLE

Your first rendezvous with a prospective companion should be simple and inexpensive. Why? Spending too much money on a first meeting is not necessary and may be counterproductive for two reasons. That first date could easily be your only date, so why drop a wad of cash? In addition, if you continue to see someone, it's difficult to rein in spending once you've set a precedent. It's far easier to upgrade from a burger joint to a steakhouse than cut back from filet mignon to a patty.

What are some good ideas for a first date? Coffee, dessert, a light lunch or a stroll in the park are excellent options. Simple outings keep the stress factor low while being kind to your budget. Dating can be an expensive proposition if not held in check.

It's also a good idea to keep first encounters rather short. When my wife and I met the first time, it was for an early lunch with no commitment to anything further. Even so, we both left the rest of the day open just in case we really hit it off. The plan worked wonderfully. We had an enjoyable day together that ended with dinner that evening. But, had it not worked out, our commitment would have only required an hour or two.

When will you know how things are going? You should be able to tell within the first 15 minutes if a date is progressing well and if you're both interested. If you really hit it off, great. Extend your time together as long as you made allowance for it. However, if you just don't "click" in person, why prolong the misery of a long date? Part ways amicably and wish each other the best.

What type of first dates should you avoid? Anything that keeps you from talking with each other. A good example of a bad first date is going to a movie. You're guaranteed about two hours of silence. Not a very positive way to start a relationship. Skip plays, concerts, comedy shows, dance clubs and bars, as well. In most cases, you should resist the temptation to plan a date where your time together will be characterized by little verbal interaction or competition with a noisy environment.

Gatherings such as weddings, graduations, reunions, birthday parties (including your own) and similar group events should also be avoided. With family and friends in attendance, such outings have awkward written all over them. Save these occasions for later in a relationship. Double dates fall into the same category.

CHOOSE APPROPRIATE ATTIRE

You've probably heard the saying, "Clothes make the man" (and, by association, woman). I believe it's true to an extent. While what you wear doesn't change who you are, it does reveal a good deal concerning you. And, though clothes can be perceived as both a reflection of status and a statement of fashion, what's important is what they divulge about an individual.

Your choice of attire should convey a positive manner. Not flash, but substance. What you wear affects how others view you with regard to at least three factors: self-confidence, when you look good, you feel good and that's perceived by others; interests, whether you're athletic and love the outdoors, are laid back and casual, or prefer a more formal atmosphere; and personal taste, good or bad. If you find yourself challenged in this regard, seek out a friend who knows how to dress well or locate an image consultant who can help improve your appearance while being true to who you are inside. You owe it to yourself to look your best. By the way, this applies to all of life, not just online dating.

In most cases, when you meet someone for the first time you should dress to impress, but in a casual fashion. Not t-shirts-and-tattered-jeans casual, but relaxed casual. It says that you're fun, approachable and easy going. Gals, you're usually way better at this than most men. Dress as you would for hanging with your girlfriends. Shoot for modest, as well. No revealing outfits, please, as they send the wrong signals. That may also apply to a lesser extent for the guys.

An exception to casual attire would be for those meeting right after work or during their lunch hour. In those cases, it's your call whether to take a change of clothes or wear what you have on. Arriving from an office job is less of an issue than from a blue-collar workplace. Regardless, aim to be presentable. If you have to apologize for your appearance, you're better off rescheduling so you look your best for an initial face-to-face.

Although not ideal for a first date, if you choose to meet for dinner, select a restaurant that offers an informal atmosphere and dress accordingly. Relaxed and business casual are appropriate attire for such an evening rendezvous, especially if you decide to go for a stroll after dinner or take part in another informal activity or event. Casual attire also tends to put you more at ease.

Please don't neglect proper grooming and physical hygiene either, as both are critical in the dating arena. While you would think it's obvious, that's not always the case. Daily showering, an effective deodorant or antiperspirant, and fresh breath should be considered the norm, not just for special occasions. Unpleasant body odor is a major turn off. So, avoid being a Pepé Le Pew.

Gals, unless your religious beliefs prohibit the use of makeup, indulge. But, don't go overboard. Balance is the key. Too little makeup and you're a plain Jane; too much and you'll resemble a theatrical performer (or worse). Think of makeup as a means of highlighting your natural beauty, rather than a way of covering up imperfections. How much makeup is too much? When attention is drawn to the makeup rather than the beauty of the one wearing it. Select a flattering hairstyle, as well. Something that's modern and complements your figure.

Guys, arrive for your date looking presentable. That means with your fingernails clean and face shaven, unless you sport facial hair. In the latter case, keep it neatly trimmed. For your hair style, choose a contemporary and fashionable look and, by all means, no toupees or combovers for the prematurely balding. Besides resembling a piece of roadkill, they scream "lack of confidence" and actually accentuate your baldness. Your potential match will see right through this visible lie.

Above all, be yourself—your best self. Fitting are the words of the Greek philosopher Epictetus. "Know, first, who you are; and then adorn yourself accordingly."

FOCUS ON POSITIVE DIALOGUE

Another first-date concern is what to discuss. Initially, you should focus on learning about each other's backgrounds, childhoods, hobbies and interests, preferences in music and movies, careers, family and friends, and religious upbringings. They're all good and predominantly safe fodder for discussion. If you tend to draw a blank easily when put on the spot, make a list of questions to ask and review them ahead of time.

Prepare your own soundbites to share in advance, brief stories about experiences you've had, interesting things you've done and anything that will make you memorable in a positive way. You want to remain in your potential mate's thoughts after the date is over. Also, do your best to not let the conversation lag. Nothing is more uncomfortable than long silences early in a relationship.

Focus on sharing your strengths and not your weaknesses. The latter will surface soon enough. Take advantage of the opportunity to sell yourself, but not in an arrogant, boastful way. Discuss your best qualities in a sincere, humble fashion.

Another bit of advice to heed, listen more than talk. It's a skill that will serve you well. Be sure to ask the questions you deem most important and share what you need to share, but make your date feel like you really care about what they have to say. Keep distractions to a minimum. Leave your cellphone in your pocket or purse and don't watch the clock. Be present in the moment.

Your date will appreciate it. Also, offer genuine compliments, but steer clear of insincerity.

What topics should you avoid? Anything negative. Leave the discussion of matters such as failed relationships, exes still in the picture, financial woes, health concerns, sensitive information, childhood issues and any bad habits until later. Unless, of course, you're asked directly about them. Even then, I suggest that you encourage your date to focus on positive topics for the present.

I'm not saying you should hide the truth. Don't be ingenuine. If your date asks a question you're not ready to address, be candid about it or decline to answer. Offer a simple reply such as, "I'll be glad to share that with you later, but today I feel it's best to discuss other things." Or, "I think that's a good question, but I'm not quite ready to share that with you."

Moreover, while it may be obvious to some, it's not always obvious to all. Don't lie. Not even a little white lie. It's dishonest, unhealthy and always comes back to haunt you. Don't bring up marriage yet either. It's a great way to send your date packing.

As a caution, it's prudent at this stage to keep your personal information to yourself. Don't divulge home or work addresses, phone numbers or email addresses. When you're reasonably sure the relationship is going well and likely to continue, you can do that. Until then, "Mum's the word!"

LEARN FROM EXPERIENCE

A first date is your opportunity to learn details about someone's personality, manners, behavior and demeanor, characteristics that are only disclosed fully in person. Note how your potential match acts toward you, and how they relate to others. Do they smile and make eye contact? Are they patient and polite? Does your date open doors for strangers, as well as for you? Or, are they rude to waiters and waitresses? Do they push their way through lines? Are they snippy or verbally abusive?

All these things will clue you in on what life will be like with your potential companion. One thing is sure. Once the newness of a relationship wears off, they'll eventually treat you the same way they treat others. So, take note (and take notes, if needed).

You should also consider your stance on concurrent dating. While I mentioned this issue before, it's worth revisiting. Can you handle dating more than one person at a time? Has that worked for you in the past? What if someone you start to date is going out with multiple partners at once? Can you accept that arrangement? Or, do you abide by the mantra "less is more" on this matter?

While some can juggle multiple relationships, others prefer not. I fell into the latter camp. When I was actively dating, I could only focus on one individual at a time. The choice, of course, is yours to make. But, if you're not dating exclusively, I suggest that you convey that fact clearly. Especially if you go beyond a first date with someone. To assume you and your match are on the same page regarding this decision is a false assumption.

ESTABLISH BOUNDARIES NOW

In the first chapter of this book, I discussed the need to establish your standards of conduct prior to dating, physical boundaries in particular. Hormones are a force to be reckoned with and the time of reckoning is never during the heat of the moment. Wait until it comes around and you'll typically exceed what you or your date is comfortable with physically. If anything has the potential to ruin a relationship before it even has a chance to blossom, it's this.

When meeting for the first time, deciding on an appropriate physical greeting can be tricky. What are you comfortable with and what is your date expecting? With what physical gestures will you conclude your rendezvous? Are you both in agreement or not? It's something worth considering in advance. Deciding the matter before you meet takes the edge off what's appropriate and what's not appropriate behavior.

First, I'll offer a qualification concerning my advice on this matter. My beliefs, as should be apparent to you by now, are conservative in nature and that's reflected in what follows. Still, I'm convinced my counsel will serve you well regardless of where you stand on the issue of appropriate physical involvement. I have reasons that we'll get to below. So, stay with me.

A smile and verbal greeting when you meet for the first time are the most suitable responses. If you've been corresponding for a while and have already developed a rapport with each other, then a hug may be appropriate. Beyond that, it's wise to reserve more intimate forms of physical expression for later in your relationship (granted there is a later). No hand holding or arms around the waist, and certainly no kissing at this stage. You've only just met.

If your first date goes well and you make it to a second, it's appropriate to indicate interest by touch. Generally, it's best for the woman to initiate this with a light touch on the forearm or hand, but for guys it's usually okay to offer a gentle touch on the shoulders or back. At the conclusion of the date, maybe a hug, a kiss on the cheek or both.

I do have one caution regarding touch. Know the messages you're sending. If you don't have a connection with someone and you have no desire in forming one, don't initiate physical contact as it expresses interest. You may not think so, but that's the idea you're conveying, especially to guys. So, unless you're actually attracted to your date, keep your hands to yourself. In today's world, we're too quick to become physical with someone we hardly know. It's not just inappropriate, but it sends the wrong signals and cheapens the experience.

I realize at this point that some of you have classified me as a prude or ultra-conservative, perhaps both. I can live with that. What I'm seeking to do is be practical given the nature of human biology, physiology and sexuality. And, I do so for your benefit.

The only guaranteed outcome you'll experience by moving too quickly in the physical realm is a loss of sound judgement. Once the fires of passion ignite, all reason goes out the window. Your thoughts will be clouded, your perspective compromised and your ability to make wise decisions will disappear like a vapor. I've encountered it myself in the past and everyone I've discussed the subject with has experienced it, too. You can always move forward to increased levels of physical contact such as holding hands, embracing and kissing, but it's nearly impossible to revert to an earlier stage. Do yourself and your date a favor and reserve deeper levels of intimate expression for later in your relationship.

I don't say this to dampen your enjoyment, but to assist you in making a wise decision regarding an extremely important matter—deciding who you marry. Two of the best gifts you can give your future spouse are a clear conscience and an undivided heart. So, be extremely careful with the degree of physical intimacy you allow in a relationship. I'm not your parent or your conscience, and I'm not by the remotest possibility God (my wife will confirm it). Nevertheless, in this day and age, I feel it's my responsibility to offer you the best advice I can muster. On a first date, the first few even, physical contact should be minimal.

CONSIDER POST-DATEM ADVICE

Given the above, how should a first date end? That's a decision best made in advance, not something to wing at the last minute. Of course, I realize not everything can be pre-planned, especially not knowing what may transpire on a date and in the moment. Still, I've always considered it a good practice to limit first dates to a simple "Goodbye" or other expression of thanks or parting.

Why? A handshake is too impersonal and a kiss too premature. A friendly hug may be warranted, but could be considered an uncomfortable gesture for some. Since many factors come to bear in choosing the right level of interaction, use common sense and always play it safe. Don't end your date on an awkward note.

When my wife and I were preparing for our first date together, to help alleviate any fears or uneasiness either of us might have experienced, I told her there would be no first-date kiss. I simply took it off the table. Neither of us had to wonder if there would be a kiss when we greeted each other or said goodnight. Instead, when we met and when we parted ways, I gave her a gentle hug. Our level of pre-date correspondence and sharing warranted that expression. It was just right for both of us.

Obviously, you'll need to figure out what's right for you and your date. However, I believe you're best served by checking your hormones at the door. It's the wise thing to do and it shows respect for others. Okay, I'm getting down off my soapbox now…at least until the next chapter.

As I put a bow on it, I can't wrap up our first-date heart-to-heart without addressing one last point. If your initial date went well, don't hesitate. Ask for a second before you part ways. It's easier and less nerve-wracking than having to call later. Plus, it will give you a quick indication if your potential companion feels the same way as you. If they're willing, make plans. If they hem and haw, suggest you call in a few days or decline your invitation, it's a clear signal their perception of your time together was different than yours. If you have any doubts regarding their interest level, ask them. It's better to know now than wonder where you stand.

CHAPTER EIGHT

GET TO THE HEART OF THE MATTER

Love is that condition in which the happiness of another person is essential to your own.

— Robert A. Heinlein

Dating is different from most of the other activities we participate in throughout our life. Many of the tasks we undertake on any given day are performed on autopilot since they don't play into our feelings. Dating, conversely, is an emotionally-charged endeavor. We're investing ourselves in the process, putting our heart on display and becoming vulnerable all in an effort to experience the love and companionship we intensely desire. Often, what we find instead is disappointment or rejection, and that's a tough pill to swallow.

Therefore, it's common to find ourselves mentally confused, emotionally battered and physically depleted. Dating can take a toll on our health, putting us at risk. Mental stress and physical exhaustion often accompany the process. Unfortunately, we're usually a contributing factor to much of our own suffering. Yet, that need not be the case. If we approach online dating with the proper attitude, a guarded heart and some common sense, we can be a victor instead of a victim.

INTERPRET UNDERLYING EMOTIONS

In the initial stages of a romance, you'll experience many different emotions. Knowing what you're feeling at any given moment may prove difficult to ascertain. Still, you can expect to encounter at least three sentiments that will tug firmly on your heartstrings: the trio of attraction, infatuation and love, in that order.

When we experience attraction, it's based primarily on external characteristics. Often referred to as love at first sight, this emotion is what initially draws us to someone else. Attributes that attract us to another person are quite specific, too, and will vary from one individual to another. However, some aspects of attraction are universal. We're drawn to those with beautiful or handsome facial features, specific hair and eye color, as well as desired height and body types. Factors can also include how someone moves and talks, as well as the way they act or dress.

We can also be attracted to intangible traits in another such as honesty, integrity, mercy, openness, sense of humor, compassion, responsibility and respectfulness. In traditional dating, many of these attributes are not apparent when meeting someone for the first time. Online dating, however, puts them on display, to a limited extent, in the profiles of our prospective matches. Still, attraction is predominantly skin deep.

Infatuation goes beyond the externals of physical attraction, although that's a part of it, and is decidedly temporary. While it has the appearance of love, romantic feelings included, it's better identified as lust or unreasoned passion. It occurs most often at the beginning of a relationship when sexual attraction is strongest. Further, it's not limited to the young alone, but can and does afflict adults equally and just as easily.

Fueled by raging hormones, infatuation can flourish very quickly in a fledgling relationship. It brings with it heightened levels of excitement and happiness, as well as a transient surge of emotions that can overwhelm us. When we're infatuated, we believe our intended is the best thing that ever happened to us. It becomes difficult to concentrate as our minds are continually preoccupied with thoughts of our partner. Things that were once important suddenly become inconsequential, we allow other relationships to be neglected, appetites wane (or increase), sleep is lost and work suffers. When in the presence of others, it's impossible to refrain from talking about our newfound love.

Yet, underlying this emotion is a possessive and selfish spirit. It's really more about ourselves and what makes us happy than it is about the object of our infatuation. Eventually, though, one of two things happen: the initial excitement of being infatuated subsides and we find ourselves somewhat less desirous of the person who once so enamored us, or infatuation transitions to love. When we reach this stage, the relationship either ends or matures respectively.

Love can be an equally powerful emotion. In fact, during the early stages of a new romance, infatuation and love bear much in common. Enough to make it difficult, on occasion, for us to know which one we're experiencing.

Similar to its short-lived counterpart, love produces romantic feelings and heightened levels of excitement. Having said that, these usually assume a lesser though more consistent intensity level. We still daydream about our love interest and are physically drawn to them, but the experience may not be as overpowering as when we're infatuated. We enjoy being together and doing things with each other as a matter of preference, yet not at the expense of everything and everyone else.

Further, our new companion becomes an important addition to our life and their needs assume a place of prominence in our heart as we both advance to a heightened, bonded level. Excitement and physical attraction exist, and can be exceedingly intense at times, but the constant highs of being infatuated are replaced with a comfortable, deepened closeness.

Love, however, extends itself beyond emotions and is equally a decision of the will. While we don't choose to be attracted or infatuated, we do choose to love. This aspect of love sets it both apart from and above attraction and infatuation. I could go into a long discourse on love from a theological perspective at this point, but I'll leave that conversation for another time. What I will do is comment briefly on the biblical words used for love and how that relates to this discussion.

EXPRESS LOVE FULLY

While we have one word for love in the English language, that we use and misuse on a regular basis, the ancient Greek language had four words to describe different types of love: eros (AIR-ose), storge (STOR-jay), philia (FILL-ee-uh), and agape (Uh-GAH-pay).

The Bible references two of these directly in the New Testament, agape and philia, while storge is employed in its negative form. Although eros doesn't actually appear in the Bible, the Hebrew equivalent does.

Eros is the Greek word used to describe the physical, sensual intimacy experienced between a husband and wife. Storge relates to natural, familial love, the tenderness and warmth experienced among family members. Philia, from which we derive the name Philadelphia (philos, "loving" and adelphos, "brother"), the city of brotherly love, is the category of love we should portray toward those around us. And, agape, the highest of the four forms of love mentioned here, that refers to the unconditional, selfless love that comes from God.

So, what do these different forms of love have to do with finding the love of your life? I'm glad you asked! Ideally, each should be present in your new relationship, two of them now and all four once you're married.

As you grow closer to your partner and your love (philia) deepens, the two of you should become best friends. That's been my experience and I hope it's yours, too. This devoted friendship kind of love is mentioned in the New Testament right after the Apostle Peter directs husbands to show consideration and respect to their wives.[1] Guys, now would be a good time to take notes.

This pre-marital phase in your relationship is also the time to begin developing a selfless, unconditional love (agape) for each other, a love that's "not self-serving"[2] but one that places the needs of your partner above your own. As basically selfish and self-centered beings, this one doesn't come naturally. To achieve this kind of love, we need to "be imitators of God."[3]

When you finally say "I do," you and your spouse form a new family unit. Once that happens, it shouldn't take long before you start to feel a growing, bonded type of familial love (storge) toward each other and toward any children that may be a part of your household. It's a yours, mine and ours experience. In biblical terms, your goal as a family is to "be devoted to one another in love" (a compound use of philia and storge).[4]

Of course, at this point you definitely want sexual intimacy (eros) to be a significant ingredient in your life. It's a natural outflow of your love for each other in all its forms. Apart from the bonding that exists in marriage, however, it's just sex, and often more about self-fulfillment than meeting the needs of another. In marriage, passionate, romantic love finds its fulfillment. If you've never read the Song of Solomon, put it on your to do list. This Old Testament book of the Bible elevates physical, marital love when experienced within the proper boundaries.

When your search is finally over and that one special love you've been seeking is a part of your life, you owe it to each other to experience this fourfold love. Don't settle for anything less.

AVOID FANTASY ISLAND

When seeking a partner online, it's not only possible but all too easy to believe you've found the love of your life based on a profile alone. This form of wishful thinking can quickly turn into planning a life together before you've even met. Unintentionally, you create a fantasy relationship in your mind and then get your hopes dashed to bits when it doesn't work out. Many surrender unwittingly to this self-deception.

How do you avoid this scenario? Recognize that until your first date, you won't know if you're a match. You may have shared considerable information with each other beforehand, but until you meet face-to-face you'll have no idea if a true connection exists between you or not. You'll also discover at this point if any objectionable quirks or peculiarities stand out. And, if your date was untruthful regarding what they shared in their profile, that will likely present itself, as well.

With that in mind, don't create expectations for a relationship in advance. Move ahead cautiously, take baby steps and shun excessive emailing, texting and talking until you've met in person. Even after that first date, guard your heart. Don't be too quick to invest yourself emotionally. Your "Wow! I'm going to marry this person" may be their "I had a nice time" or, worse, "I'm glad this date is over." Truthfully, you could have what you thought were several great dates together and still get a "Dear John" or "Dear Jane" phone call, email or text. Possibly, no word at all.

Of course, that's all easier said than done. I've had my fair share of heartbreaks over the years from relationships that didn't quite live up to my high expectations. Many times, all it took was one date plus some serious fantasizing on my part (I'm referring to wholesome fantasies) to set the gears in motion, creating hopes around a relationship that wasn't a relationship at all. So, guard your thoughts. It takes a great deal of effort to keep the roller coaster of fantasy from becoming a perceived reality in a relationship that's severely one-sided.

If we're truthful with ourselves, we've been guilty of moving too fast on more than one occasion in our lives. In many cases, we're just lonely and want to share our life with someone else. Or, we may have a raging libido and are seeking an appropriate outlet. It could be that the clock is ticking because we're getting older and still want to start a family. Sometimes, we sense a void and believe that another person can fill it (a subject that we covered earlier). More likely, it's a combination of the above.

Real relationships take time and patience to develop, growing stronger with the seasons of life and from shared experiences. I know waiting can be hard, especially when you're tired of dating and want desperately to find the love of your life. But, moving too fast and getting your hopes up too quickly are unwise on many counts. Plus, you're likely to scare someone off in the process.

Nonetheless, hope is essential to life—hope for a better future, hope for answered prayer and hope we'll eventually find love that lasts a lifetime. In the book of Proverbs, we're told "Hope deferred makes the heart sick, but a longing fulfilled is a tree of life."[5] Those words emphasize the life-giving nature of hope. Just don't confuse it with wishful thinking. Hope keeps us going through difficult times; wishful thinking leaves us wanting.

BEWARE EMOTIONAL INVESTMENTS

Maybe you haven't created a fantasy-based relationship, but what about that winsome guy or cute gal who hasn't responded to your smiles, winks or questions? Maybe they did respond, but with a "Not interested." Has it put you in a funk? Did it leave you feeling depressed? If so, you're emotionally over-invested.

Of course, being ignored or rejected is disappointing. That's natural. Still, it shouldn't ruin your day or week. Nor should it cause despair. Reasons abound for not receiving a response from someone. It could be they're not currently active on the service.

Perhaps they only signed up to casually look around, are too busy with work to respond or are already in a relationship.

What if you find yourself bending over backwards trying to win someone's attention and affection. Or, maybe you're willing to sacrifice non-negotiables to gain a relationship? If that's the case, you're not just over-invested emotionally, you're likely dealing with impatience or low self-esteem, as well. The simple truth, not that it's simple to apply, is that you need to value yourself enough to keep your needs on an equal plane with those of whomever you date and eventually marry. Growing, healthy relationships are evidenced by reciprocal giving and taking.

Regardless, if you find the above to be true, it may be a good idea to take a dating hiatus to evaluate why you're expending so much emotional energy. Is past rejection causing you to over-invest? Has a lack of success caused feelings of desperation? What about self-confidence? Is it at an all-time low? Whatever's causing you to overcompensate in this area, I suggest stepping back from dating for a time so you can deal with it. As I commented earlier, make sure you're healthy before seeking a new relationship.

BALANCE HORMONES AND NEURONS

On this next point, many of you will likely disagree with me, but that's okay. You won't hurt my feelings. What I'm sharing is not for my benefit, but yours.

While sex is an extremely important aspect of marriage, sexual compatibility before your nuptials is not. Don't misunderstand me. I'm not saying that you shouldn't discuss sexual preferences before you get married. It's an important topic. But, having sex before marriage is counter-productive. It can lead to distrust and have negative repercussions if your relationship doesn't work out, and potentially even if it does. Physical intimacy also increases the odds that you won't make wise, clear-headed decisions. To put it another way, hormones can make you stupid. Once the fires of passion ignite, everything changes.

Furthermore, the phrases "sexual compatibility" and "sexually compatible" are really misnomers in the context where they're traditionally applied. What most people mean when using these terms is that their sexual encounter with a given person was either good, bad or just average. It's a perception regarding how much they enjoyed the experience.

True sexual compatibility doesn't just happen, but is nurtured through an ongoing process. In marriage, a couple continues to "flesh out" their sexual experience for the purpose of making it more pleasurable and fulfilling for each other. Before you walk down the aisle, however, you only need to ascertain whether or not your sexual preferences are compatible. That only requires discussion, not a roll in the sack.

Not only is sex before marriage a bad idea, but the same is true for cohabitation. Living together is an open-ended contract with a built-in escape clause in case things "don't work out." No true commitment exists in a relationship of that nature. You're seeking love for a lifetime, not a free trial program or the offer of a money-back guarantee. Among other essentials, loyalty, faithfulness and fidelity are lacking apart from the commitment marriage brings.

In addition, those of faith know that the Bible instructs us that God intended sex to be enjoyed only in the context of marriage, between one man and one woman, as a safeguard designed to protect us, not a directive intended to confine us.[6] Throughout the Bible we're taught to avoid all forms of sexual immorality,[7] we're required to honor our bodies as sacred[8] and not exclusively our own,[9] and we're constrained in all of our thoughts, conduct and decisions to exhibit the principle of love, seeking the best interests of others. That means you need to place your future spouse's welfare, long-term and short, above your own, protecting and respecting them in the process.[10]

Apart from Judeo-Christian values and the biblical reasons for reserving sexual intimacy for marriage, practical considerations support that decision, as well. It limits your exposure to disease, prevents unplanned pregnancy, reduces stress and guilt, and rewards commitment. According to a study related via *WebMD*, several marital benefits have relevance to those who choose to wait. Findings suggest that "…couples who wait until marriage are happier with the quality of sex than couples who have intercourse before their vows. What's more, couples who delay sex until their wedding night have more stable and happier marriages than couples who have premarital sex."[11]

So, hold off on sexual intimacy until you're married. Reap the benefits of delayed gratification and keep as many of your brain cells alive and fully functioning for as long as possible.

MAINTAIN A POSITIVE ATTITUDE

As with conventional dating, searching for love online can often be a hurtful and disappointing experience. With few exceptions, rejection is a given. If it hasn't occurred yet, prepare yourself for the inevitable. Even when it seems like you've made a genuine connection, being rejected is still possible. No one is immune to it either. The best advice I can offer to you, as with anything worth attaining in life, is to stick with it and strive your best to maintain a positive attitude.

Also, be assured that rejection isn't personal, at least not before you've met face-to-face. Based solely on your profile and early correspondence, someone may reject you for all the right reasons or for all the wrong ones. It's something you have little control over apart from making sure that nothing in your profile is scaring potential matches away.

Many suggest that dating is strictly a numbers game. Date enough people, suffer enough rejections and you'll eventually find your soulmate. Sounds depressing, doesn't it? Others have concluded it's simply a matter of faith, trusting God to bring your significant other to you. I believe the truth lies somewhere in a balance between the two. You do your part and God does his. While some may doubt it, God really does want what's best for us as echoed in the words of the prophet Jeremiah. "'For I know the plans I have for you,' declares the Lord, 'plans to prosper you and not to harm you, plans to give you hope and a future.'"[12]

Notwithstanding, don't be surprised if those plans involve some waiting and a lot of dating. Finding your significant other could take weeks, months or years. If you give up too soon, however, you'll never find that special someone.

CHAPTER NINE

NEVER GIVE UP

I have learned not to worry about love; but to honor its coming with all my heart.

—*Alice Walker*

When you've given online dating your best effort and you still find yourself eating dinner and watching movies alone, what should you do? It could be that you've tried several dating services so far without success. It's likely you've gone on dozens of dates (or more) and not found a compatible match. It's possible you've even read a stack of books, bought an online course or hired a dating consultant and you've still come up with empty hands and an empty heart.

You may have even asked yourself, and possibly God, if there's hope, "Is it worth continuing this search or am I doomed to a life of singleness?" I'll respond by echoing an oft-repeated line from the movie *Galaxy Quest* starring Tim Allen. In his leading role as

Commander Peter Quincy Taggert, Allen valiantly retorts, "Never Give Up, Never Surrender!"

TRY, TRY AGAIN

Let's be honest. Online dating, for many singles, is arduous. It requires significant time and effort to complete personality tests, create profiles and then sift through hundreds of possible matches searching for prospective partners who offer the best chance of compatibility. It's often a painful experience, as well. Rejection is a close companion to the dating process, and even more so with Internet dating where it just takes the click of a mouse or a short message to tell someone, "Not interested!"

Success doesn't come quickly for most singles either. According to a recent *Consumer Reports* article based on a group of 9,600 respondents, 15 percent had been dating online for an average of four to six months, 17 percent six months to a year, another 17 percent one to two years and 21 percent for two years or longer. Only 28 percent had been dating for less than three months. The good news, however, is that 44 percent of those surveyed, close to half, have had or are currently involved in a "serious long-term relationship or have gotten married."[1] Unfortunately, many online daters quit too soon.

So, don't give up! That's the first bit of advice I'll offer. Consider the old adage, "If at first you don't succeed, try, try again." It's certainly appropriate for anyone who has dabbled with online dating, any dating for that matter. In most cases, persistence does pay off. Maybe not today or tomorrow, but eventually. You just need to stick with it.

FIX WHAT'S BROKEN

So, what's next if you experience a lack of success? Note that I didn't say failure. You only fail if you choose to quit. Nonsuccess simply means that you haven't found the right person yet. All the same, if others aren't contacting you and no one's responding to your attempts at communicating with them, it's not an accident. Something's wrong, but it's not necessarily you. The solution may be as simple as tweaking your profile.

My suggestion? Re-read the chapter, Create a Winning Profile, and page through your bio again, but with a critical eye this time. Better yet, have a friend or family member look it over with you. Someone who will be honest about anything you've included that might be turning others away. Then, revise it and make it shine! Don't "modify" the truth, but ensure that your profile reflects a positive attitude and that it shows you in the best possible light. You might want to change your profile name, as well, if the site you've chosen employs them.

If you're using a service that sends you daily matches and the well is running dry, it may be time to broaden your search criteria. I'm not suggesting that you compromise on anything important. Rather, increase the distance you're willing to travel or tweak your age or height requirements a bit. You may want to consider dating someone from a different ethnicity, as well.

Have you been too confining in your preferences? Are blond hair and blue eyes a make-or-break proposition? What about a slender figure or toned abs? Ideals are okay, but don't let them limit your pool of available matches. Be less restrictive. A terrific match could be waiting just outside your current parameters.

Expanding on the above, I'll offer this next bit of advice with care. You may need to adjust your expectations. No, I'm not suggesting that you throw out your non-negotiables. However, you may need to take a hard look at your standards and reassess them. Realize that potential matches with amazing profiles may not be amazing in person. Conversely, those with average or below-average online bios could end up being exceptional. Put another way, you might not have to kiss any frogs to find your prince or princess, but at least be willing to pucker up.

Also, consider changing up your photos. It's possible the ones you originally chose aren't working to your advantage. Did you use selfies, group shots or pictures with your ex cut off? What about professional photographs? If you didn't have them taken before, now would be an ideal time to arrange a photo shoot and replace those old pictures with new, flattering shots. Don't chintz here. Your photographs have more to do with making a great first impression than any other element in your profile. So, if you can't afford to hire a professional, find someone in your circle of family or friends who's a good photographer and have them take some new pictures. It's really worth the time and expense!

Finally, if you're not having success with the dating site you've chosen and none of the above changes make a difference, it's time to check out another service and get exposed to a different pool of matches. If you've been using a paid service, take one of the free ones for a spin. If you're on a free service, now would be a good time to invest in a paid site for at least three months to see if you achieve better results.

Frequently, a change of environment does us all good in life. In this case, you may benefit by giving another audience the chance to view some new scenery—you.

ADDRESS PHYSICAL ISSUES

I know what I'm about to say can sting a bit, but the problem may not be your profile. While what's on the inside counts most over the long haul, perceptions matter. Just as the value of a book is often judged by its cover, so people are frequently appraised at the outset by their appearance. Unfortunate, but true.

Sometimes we need to take an honest and perhaps painful look at ourselves to establish if we're dealing with any outward physical issues or personality flaws. I'm not bringing up this subject to be cruel, but to offer you the best chance of success in your dating efforts. Address the following if necessary and don't let yourself be eliminated from the equation before you even have a chance to show others why you would make a great companion.

While certain characteristics like body type, glandular issues, physical deformities and handicaps are difficult, if not impossible, to alter, things like poor grooming and personal hygiene are easily remedied. Please refer to the previous chapter, Practice First-Date Etiquette, if you need a refresher on this matter. For now, let's focus on what you can do to improve your appearance with a modest amount of effort.

First, let's consider a few things you can remedy on your own or with a little outside assistance. Guys, sport a current hairstyle, one that shows you care about your appearance. Gals, if you've got unruly hair, don't just put on a hat. It's time to see a stylist. Maybe you need a new hairstyle or better haircare products. Also, while I'm not a fan of wigs, they're often the best option for women with severely thinning hair. But, go for quality if you do. Good wigs are hard to distinguish from the real thing.

Speaking of hair, ladies, if you're sporting an excess amount on your face, please attend to it. Don't worry about that peach fuzz you can barely see. It's the prominent facial hair that need to be addressed. In other words, while a mustache and sideburns can be dashing on a man (at least back in the 70s), gals just can't pull them off. And please, don't physically pull them off. Waxing is fine on a car, not so much on your face. Just a guy's perspective. Use a gentler product instead, a cream or facial hair remover. Tweeze those eyebrows, too, if necessary.

Are you challenged when it comes to applying makeup? Now might be a good time to schedule an appointment with a friend who's talented with cosmetic application or meet with a beauty consultant. Learn new techniques to bring out the beauty that's present, but hidden. Do you struggle with complexion issues? See a dermatologist. You may have a treatable skin condition. This applies to men, as well.

Although this next point is a rather touchy one, it's something I can't neglect to mention. If you have any correctable facial defects, even minor ones, deal with them now. I'm not suggesting facelifts, Botox injections or elective procedures to remove signs of age. I'm referring specifically to cosmetic treatment for scars and the surgical removal of moles, though other fleshy growths like warts and skin tags apply.

Facial scars and severe acne damage can take a toll on your confidence and self-esteem, as well as make it difficult to connect with potential matches. I'm not a medical professional, so I won't take it upon myself to give you any advice on what procedures to perform or products to use. Still, I do know that many options exist for correcting or improving complexion issues and it's in your best interest to consider them.

With regard to moles, I'm not talking about small, flat moles on the cheek or adjacent to the lips that could be considered beauty marks. I'm zeroing in on larger moles, with or without hairs, that immediately draw attention and cause people to stare or look away. No debate, these facial protrusions need to go. Not only do they detract from your appearance, but they pose a potential cancer risk. Okay, I've said it. I hope you're not offended.

With regard to your body as a whole, it may be time to address excessive weight or other health-related issues. See your family doctor and get a full physical. Work on a plan with him or her to improve your health. Consult a dietician if needed and a personal trainer if you lack the discipline to exercise regularly. At the very least, find someone to be your workout buddy and help keep you accountable. Consistent exercise and a change in diet may do more for you than simply shaving off a few pounds. It could drastically improve your overall health, make you feel better in general, improve your outlook and bolster your confidence.

Of course, I realize several of the above suggestions can be costly and that many of you simply can't afford to address them all at once. That's alright. Start by picking one improvement you can implement now. You can deal with the others later.

MAKE ATTITUDE ADJUSTMENTS

In addition to the appearance issues already addressed, we also need to examine attitudes. Once again, I'm going to be honest with you. Some of you need an attitude adjustment. If you belong to the school of thought that embraces a "that's how I am and you need to accept it" mentality, it's time to be re-educated.

Regrettably, I've met many individuals over the years that spout that twisted belief and it's simply unacceptable. It comes across as self-righteous, patronizing and obnoxious. The sooner it's ditched and replaced with a positive orientation the better.

Some folks don't even realize that their attitude is keeping love at bay. It's unfortunate, but true. Espousing that viewpoint is just an excuse for those not wanting to change and mature as a person or a mechanism to avoid dealing with underlying issues. Whether based on laziness, insecurity, impatience or low self-worth, it's a self-defeating mindset. Sadly, if you're reading this and you suffer from such a deficiency, you'll probably be offended by what I've just shared. You'll think that you're being misunderstood, judged unfairly and go on denying the need of an attitude overhaul. I hope that I'm wrong and that you'll discuss it with a trusted friend or counselor. Either way, I wish you the best.

SURVIVE DATING BURNOUT

Initially, online dating can be exciting and adventurous, though I've heard a few singles refer to it as fearful and frustrating. Still, six months to a year down the road and all your exuberance and hopefulness can degenerate into boredom and discouragement, just another item to check off your daily to-do list. If that's the case, then you're dealing with dating burnout and that leaves you with several options. Giving up, as mentioned at the beginning of this chapter, is not one of them.

First, you can continue your present dating routine and increase the burn out. Obviously, that's not a choice I recommend. The better alternative is to take a break from online dating to regroup and reenergize—a few days, several weeks, a month or longer. It all depends on how bad the burnout is that you're experiencing.

So, instead of spending yet another lonely evening or weekend pouring through a fresh batch of possible matches, do something nice for yourself. No, don't go on a spending spree. Invest some time in a simple activity or hobby you enjoy. Read a book, catch a movie, take a walk in the park or pamper yourself a bit. Or, join some friends for coffee or dessert. The real-world interaction will do you good and will help you brush up on your relational skills. Devote the time necessary to relax and make yourself feel good. That's all there is to it.

You have another option, too. Try some "old-school" dating for a change of pace. Yes, it's still dating, but in a different setting that gets you away from the virtual world you've been inhabiting. A friend of a friend, a newcomer where you worship, even someone you've run into several times at the grocery store are all potential matches. Keep your eyes open to the opportunities around you.

Whatever option you choose, you'll likely discover that your timeout was exactly what you needed to alleviate the weariness. While not a cure-all, taking a break can lessen the pressure tied to finding that special someone, and that itself is often the best reason. Afterward, you can resume dating online with a refreshed perspective and recharged emotions.

ANTICIPATE UNSEEN GUIDANCE

Once you've done everything feasible to ensure you're ready to date with the greatest chance of success, put forth the daily effort needed to achieve the desired results. It's that due-diligence factor again. Still, those of faith know they're not alone in this process. Every aspect in the search for the love of your life needs to be considered in light of this truth. Again, I know I may lose some of you here and in the paragraphs below, but I firmly believe that what I'm sharing is critical to your endeavors.

If you think you're alone in your search for a life partner, you're already disadvantaged. Whereas, believers in God know they're not on their own as they seek a soulmate. When you bathe your online dating efforts in prayer and trust God to guide you, it offers tremendous security and hope—two commodities that are sorely needed in the often discouraging, disheartening and exhausting process of finding the love of a lifetime.

Not sure what to believe? Examine your heart. As you do, I think you'll discover more than just a strong desire to share your life with someone special. I'm confident you'll sense, at your core, that you're seeking to fill an even greater need. I challenge you to be open to experiencing something, Someone, beyond yourself. Honestly, what do you have to lose? You certainly have everything to gain.

PLAY THE WAITING GAME

For those who place their trust in God, as well as those new to the experience, don't lose heart. We all have seasons of waiting, times when he doesn't seem to answer us. No matter how often it happens, the experience never seems to get easier. We live in a society characterized by microwaves, fast food, digital cameras, instant messaging and streaming entertainment. But, God seldom works instantly in our lives. Waiting is usually involved.

Before I met Deb on eHarmony, I experienced a long season of silence that lasted about four years. I prayed and read my Bible daily, actively served in ministry, listened intently for an answer… and nothing came. It was, quite frankly, a struggle to press on and believe God was still at work in my life, a time when I battled depression and anxiety every day. All I could do was hang on and trust in spite of my circumstances. Eventually, the pieces slowly began to fall into place and I started to see how God had been directing my steps. The path before me wasn't entirely clear yet, but I knew the silence was coming to end. Eventually, I was able to understand, at least in part, what God had been doing all along.

Of course, the key is to trust even when it's difficult and doesn't make sense. We have a loving God who is concerned about what happens in our lives, as well as how we respond to it all. He is with us whether we feel his presence or not. In the online dating sphere, as well as all areas of life, God plays a part. And, a big one at that.

I trust you'll take these words to heart. Knowing that you're not alone in your singleness and in the search for a spouse makes all the difference. In fact, it can be the difference between hope and hopelessness.

In the midst of your waiting, I leave you with the charge to be patient. Times of discouragement and disappointment will likely come your way, but if you stick with it, so will the opportunity to find the love of your life. And, that's worth the wait!

CHAPTER TEN

CONFIRM IT'S A MATCH

Love is patient, love is kind. It does not envy, it does not boast, it is not proud. It does not dishonor others, it is not self-seeking, it is not easily angered, it keeps no record of wrongs. Love does not delight in evil but rejoices with the truth. It always protects, always trusts, always hopes, always perseveres. Love never fails.

—Apostle Paul[1]

If all of your hard work and diligence has finally paid off and you've met that special someone, the One you've been longing to find, "Congratulations!" That was a principal goal of mine in writing this book.

However, if you haven't discovered that special someone just yet, earmark this page and return to it when you have. Either way, I want to share a few final thoughts for your consideration before you say "I do."

CONFIRM IT'S A MATCH

ACCEPT GOOD ADVICE

Whatever happens, don't settle. No one benefits in the long run when you do. This should be self-evident, but the heart has a way of justifying almost anything or anyone. If you have doubts about your feelings, make excuses for your partner's attitudes or actions, are forging ahead against the advice of family and friends, or find yourself defending the relationship in any way, you need to step back and reassess you and your partner as a couple. Determine if it's truly a match made in heaven or if it feels more like it originated in, well, a toastier climate.

Honestly, if you're in a relationship that doesn't truly excite you and bring joy to your heart, you haven't met the love of your life. You owe it to yourself to continue your search. Otherwise, the result will be two hurt and lonely people stuck together, with the potential for children who become collateral damage. If you think you're unhappy being alone, it's nothing compared to finding out that you married the wrong person.

Moreover, be careful to avoid the "I really don't deserve more" or "this may be my last chance" mindsets. You deserve the best, which is also the best for your partner. Your good is their good. As for a last chance, that only happens if you give up too soon.

Have you observed any indicators that your relationship isn't all it should be? If so, you need to consider those warning signs carefully. Watch for uncomfortable silences, an unforgiving spirit, chronic criticism, daily tension, uncontrolled arguments, frequent defensiveness, evidence of dishonesty and a lack of respect, trust and acceptance. Other signs exist, as well, but you get the idea. If your relationship is characterized by negative attributes rather than positive ones, discuss it with your partner or take a timeout. Actually, consider both.

So, given the above, how do you know if you've found the One? A "litmus test"[2] exists to aid you in making that assessment.

TAKE THE LITMUS TEST

Although no one else can tell you if you've found the right guy or gal, and while no barometer of crucial indicators is foolproof, the guidelines below can assist in confirming whether or not you've found your special someone. Not all of these gauges may be true of your relationship at the moment, but the majority should be a part of your shared experience. In no particular order, they are...

YOU'RE LOVED FOR BEING YOU

You know you've met the One when you're loved for who you are, imperfections and all. On good days or bad, dolled up or disheveled, clean-cut or unshaven, playful or reclusive, you don't have to hide a thing from your partner because they love and accept you along with all the qualities that make you so unique. Serious or silly, it doesn't matter. Nor do you have to impress them. You've already done that by being you. What's more, they make you feel good about yourself.

YOU HAVE A NEW BEST FRIEND

The best relationships are based on true friendship and shared respect. You enjoy being with your companion above being with anyone else. You not only love each other, but you like each other, as well. When a new movie comes out, you'll want to see it with your partner. On a beautiful day, you'll desire to share it together outdoors. You know how they feel and what's on their mind, and vice versa. You also function as a team, help each other with the smallest of chores and run errands jointly just so you can be close. You've realized that your relationship and friendship have become top priorities in life.

FAMILY AND FRIENDS ARE RESPECTED

Everyone has their quirks. Your family and friends aren't excluded either (really, they're not). Nonetheless, your intended respects and appreciates them. In fact, he or she may even grow to love them and enjoy spending time with them. But, if not, he or she will buck up for your sake and endure because they're your relatives and besties. Since your friends and family are important to you, they're important to your partner. That reminds me of a girl I dated in college. She didn't like my friends, not one of them. That should have tipped me off early on that she wasn't a suitable match, but I was blinded by love. A relationship of that nature is cursed from the start. Don't repeat my error.

OTHERS ENCOURAGE YOUR RELATIONSHIP

Sometimes it's wise to ignore the advice of your family and friends when it comes to relationships, especially if you're being pushed reluctantly into one. Most of the time, however, you should listen carefully to what they have to say about your intended companion. If the people you trust the most, those who love you and care about what happens to you, plead with you to distance yourself from your current partner, strongly consider their heartfelt counsel. Conversely, if they encourage the relationship, you should accept that as positive reinforcement.

CONFLICT IS MANAGED WELL

A couple that doesn't have disagreements or arguments either hasn't been together long, or one or both parties aren't being totally honest with the other. Needs and wants aren't being voiced or addressed. Eventually, paradise will be tainted as conflict is inevitable. What matters is how it's handled when it comes.

Your partner won't belittle or seek to manipulate you, hold a grudge or drag out an argument. They'll recognize you're only human, as they are, and that sometimes frustration and stress get the better of you. Healthy conflict results in a greater respect for each other and serves to strengthen a relationship, while temper tantrums, personal insults, slamming doors, throwing objects or worse, emotional and physical abuse, all damage a relationship.

Well-managed conflict is also evidenced by minimal or non-existent drama. When arguments arise, each party does their best to listen carefully, fight fair, acknowledge each other's good points, admit when they're wrong and then apologize. Constant drama is a sign something's wrong and that the one you're with may not be the One you've been dreaming about.

YOUR GOALS IN LIFE MATCH

Compatibility is the key to developing long-term relationships with a deep, enduring connection. When goals are in sync, that's a huge plus. Once you find the love of your life, planning and preparing for the future will be a positive experience. Formulating life and career goals together will enrich your relationship.

On the other hand, if your goals are dissimilar, then the two of you will have a lessened possibility of long-term fulfillment and enjoyment as a couple. If, for instance, you're a minimalist and enjoy the simple things in life while your partner's top priority is making money and accumulating possessions, beware! The same holds true if you want kids, but your partner doesn't. Make sure early on that your crucial goals are compatible.

YOU DEEPLY RESPECT ONE ANOTHER

A relationship lacking respect is ill-fated. It's a critical element in a healthy, growing marriage. When mutual respect abounds, you have the best chance of building a solid foundation for a deep and secure connection. That involves not just loving someone, but liking them, as well. When that's the case, trust increases, communication steadily improves, all aspects of your relationship flourish and your satisfaction level skyrockets.

The right partner will consider your needs as a priority and be supportive of your dreams, even if time and money are scarce. They'll adjust their schedule and expectations for your benefit. However, if a lack of respect exists on the part of one or both partners, it's simply a matter of time before everything implodes.

YOU'RE COMFORTABLE BEING TOGETHER

When you're completely relaxed around your partner, you're at ease being yourself. No need to dress up all the time, shave every day, maintain muss-free hair or layer on the makeup. You're as comfortable lounging around in your sweats as you are decking yourself out for a night on the town. Your partner loves, accepts and appreciates you either way. Of course, that's no excuse to be a proverbial slob around them and let your appearance go, or to be unrestrained with bodily noises even though you know they'll eventually be a part of daily life.

You're okay with silence, too. You don't have to talk all the time or feel awkward when you have nothing to say. It's okay to be quiet. In fact, you feel at ease whether you're talking or not. If that's not true, underlying fears or expectations may be dictating your actions and attitude. If you can't be relaxed together, you need to ask yourself why.

YOU KNOW WHAT MAKES EACH OTHER HAPPY

When you've found the love of your life, you're eager to discover what makes them happy, including what they want and need in life. What's more, they're eager to do likewise. Hence, it begs the question, "Do you know how to please your companion?" What brightens their day and makes them smile? What do they enjoy most in life? Do you know their preferred foods and restaurants, likes and dislikes in entertainment, and favorite holidays, sports, hobbies and activities? Are there certain places that hold a special fondness in their memory?

On a deeper level, are you aware of what causes and relieves stress in their lives, how to lift them out of the doldrums caused by personal struggles and work-related issues, as well as being able to recognize when something's troubling them? On the flip side, is that awareness reciprocal? If so, it's a good indicator that your partner is the One.

YOU WANT TO SHARE EVERYTHING

When something good happens, who's the first person you want to tell? Is it your partner? Do you think of them immediately? The same is true when you receive bad news or experience difficulties. Are they first on your mind to discuss what's happening? That's how it should be.

If your partner sincerely loves you, they'll want to share in your happiness and encourage you in your losses, difficulties and failures. You'll want to do the same for them, too. And, if you're not available in person to share what's on your heart, you'll use your computer, tablet or smartphone to call, email or text each other multiple times a day, even if it's just to say "I love you!"

Further, the little things in life also matter when you truly love and respect someone. In other words, what could be considered somewhat ordinary or mundane about life becomes interesting instead. You enjoy looking at old photos together and watching family movies to discover even the smallest details about your partner's life. Stories from their childhood and the years before you met hold a special fascination in your heart. Even what happens at work matters to you because it affects them. A lack of interest is cause for concern.

PHYSICAL AFFECTION COMES NATURALLY

If your partner finds it difficult to show physical affection or you have problems in this respect, something's not right. Cuddling, kissing and hugging should all flow comfortably and naturally between you and the love of your life. In fact, you should both find it difficult to keep your hands off each other.

When that's not true, when romantic excitement is lacking, it should raise a cautionary flag. I'm not saying you should constantly mimic a pair of octopi. However, if showing affection is forced in any way, it bears some examination. A consistent desire to express affection is a positive sign that your relationship is a good one, at least in the physical realm, and that should make you feel both secure and happy.

YOU EXPERIENCE A DEEP CONNECTION

You used to think in terms of "Where do I want to go?" and "What do I want to do?" Everything is viewed now in relation to "we" instead of "I" and an importance is attached to how the choices you make affect your partner. You're willing to change your plans, as much as possible, to adapt to their needs.

When you have to work late or go on a business trip, you're concerned how it will impact him or her. You'll leave a gathering early or not even go if your partner is sick or simply tired and wants to stay in for the evening. And, when talking with others, you'll find yourself referring to things as "ours" rather than "mine" or "theirs." If that's not the case, if you or your companion have a disconnect, you haven't reached this stage in your relationship.

ANALYZE THE RESULTS

Okay, it's time to examine your "test results" and gauge the health of your relationship based on the above criteria—before you find yourself at the altar making a life-long commitment. Review these indicators to help determine whether or not you've found the love you so desire. If each is true of your relationship, at least most of the above, you owe it to yourself to nurture your romance and allow it to become everything it's meant to be.

If, instead, your relationship misses the mark, it's time to re-evaluate whether you've really found the One or if they're just one of many on the way to connecting with the love of your life.

Another helpful means of gauging compatibility is through a study that assists you in determining if you and your companion really are a good match. One such tool to consider is *Before You Save the Date: 21 Questions to Help You Marry with Confidence* by Dr. Paul Friesen. My wife and I worked through this book study together during our time dating and found it helpful in spurring discussions regarding personal convictions, character issues and matters of compatibility. I believe it would be helpful to you, as well. If you're interested in knowing more about it, you'll find a review[3] on the *Discovering Love Online* website.

EPILOGUE

Online dating is a journey. Hopefully, a grand one as you pursue the love of your life. You'll encounter twists and turns along the way, to be sure. Roadblocks and detours are likely, as well. Just don't let them impede your progress or cause you to turn back. Your goal, to find lasting love, is much too important to postpone or abandon.

What's required to find love that lasts a lifetime? Are careful planning, hard work and unwavering tenacity the sole ingredients of success? Is it dependent on how much effort you personally expend? Or, is the outcome determined by divine guidance and provision? The answer, I believe, is that each of these factors play a crucial part in the process of finding your soulmate. It's not an either-or proposition, but a joint partnership.

As you're well aware, you can't force someone else to love you. It just doesn't work that way. They either choose to love you on their own or they don't. It's their decision entirely.

Nor can you compel anyone to choose your profile over the thousands of others available online. That's where faith enters into the picture. You do your part to be successful in your search for love and continue doing it until your goal is achieved, just as you would with any worthy endeavor. At the same time, you trust God to do his part and leave the outcome in his hands. It's as we're told in the book of Proverbs, "We can make our plans, but the Lord determines our steps."[1]

While I can't guarantee success if you follow the advice I've offered, I can promise that you'll stand out from the crowd and maximize your chance of finding love. It's really not that difficult once you have the tools and know-how required.

It's been said that two goals exist in life. One is to reach our destination and the other is to enjoy the journey. Assigning too much emphasis to one will ruin the other.[2] So, plan to achieve your goal, but enjoy the adventure while you're on it.

I genuinely hope that you found *Discovering Love Online: Love May Be Closer Than You Think* valuable and encouraging in your pursuit of lasting love. Further, I trust that you gained the counsel needed to avoid many of the pains and pitfalls of learning from your own mistakes, that the anxiety and stress so many face with online dating were lessened and that you garnered the confidence necessary to move forward with great success in your search for love. That's my sincerest wish and prayer for you.

I'll leave you with a final thought. Discovering love online, the experience not the book, is not only about your search for love, as important as that may be. It's also about imparting that gift to someone else—your future spouse. When you bless another, you make their world a better place and are blessed in return.

In your search for the love of your life, may hope be strong, grace plentiful and love abounding.

Enjoy the Adventure!

Chuck Miller

POSTSCRIPT

I f you enjoyed *Discovering Love Online: Love May Be Closer Than You Think* and found it helpful, please leave a review on Amazon.[1] Investing a few minutes of your time to write a short evaluation would be greatly appreciated. Thanks!

Also, as a brief aside, in the book's Prologue you read the tale of Brett and Brianna. You did read it, right? Well, just in case you haven't figured it out yet, that's actually the story of how Deb and I met. Our caricatures are featured on the book cover, as well, lovingly crafted by artist and friend, André Jolicoeur.[2]

APPENDIX

Though still too early to provide definitive results from the Discovering Love Online Internet Dating Survey, several interesting trends can be shared at present. First, twice as many women have taken the survey as men. That correlates to a larger pool of women seeking a partner through online dating in general. Also, over 50 percent of those choosing to date online list their marital status as divorced, a number representative of the overall divorce rate in this country.

Another observation is that the majority of survey respondents listed misrepresentation as their greatest concern when dating online. That coincides with data provided by the Pew Research Center as referenced earlier, indicating that 54 percent of online daters believe someone else seriously misrepresented themselves in their dating profile.

It's also clear from current results that the majority of those completing the survey have used a paid service at some point in their online dating experience, while the use of online dating apps among respondents is basically nil. The latter point, I believe, is indicative of the fact that standalone dating apps tend to be used primarily for casual dating rather than to find lasting love.

When more conclusive data is available from the survey, I'll update this material to reflect it, as well as post the results on the *Discovering Love Online* website.

AUTHOR BIO

Author of *Discovering Love Online: Love May Be Closer Than You Think*, architect and founder of indie publishing house Propeller Cap, LLC[1] and a former singles ministry director, Chuck Miller brings a diverse career background and nearly four decades of experience as a journalist, editor, publisher and pastor to his written portfolio.

His literary creations span technology to theology, while as a leader Chuck gained extensive experience in Christian ministry filling numerous volunteer and vocational roles. He has served on pastoral staff at several churches, invested over 20 years working with single adults of all ages and assisted as a facilitator in grief recovery support groups. His educational achievements include certifications in graphic art and photography, and Associate of Arts, Bachelor of Science and Master of Divinity degrees.

Chuck dated "religiously" as a young adult through conventional dating venues of the day. And, following a twelve-year quest for love and companionship, he enjoyed nearly 23 years of marriage before his first wife died of cancer.

In the autumn of 2014, Chuck and Deb found each other on eHarmony. Neither realized when filling out their profiles how soon it would lead them to Discovering Love Online.

After a season of healing, Chuck engaged in a four-year stint of dating the "old-fashioned" way. When that proved unproductive, he decided it was time to investigate the online alternative. As a result, Chuck and his lovely sweetheart, Deb, met on eHarmony in 2014 and married the following year. His research, experiences and success are outlined in this book as a testimony to the value of online dating and of its benefits to those who are still seeking the love of their life.

Chuck and Deb Miller live south of Cleveland, Ohio with her daughters, Dani and Carol. When Chuck's not taking a break from his daily routine to photograph nature and other subjects that pique his creativity, you'll find him working from home authoring books, writing blog posts and designing websites.

DISCOVERING LOVE ONLINE

Website: discoveringloveonline.com
Facebook: /DiscoveringLoveOnline
Facebook Community: /groups/DiscoveringLoveOnline
Instagram: /DiscoveringLoveOnline
Twitter: /DiscoverLoveOn
#DiscoveringLoveOnline

CHUCK MILLER

Website: chuckmiller.org
Facebook: /ChuckMiller.org
Facebook Community: /groups/ChuckMiller.org
Instagram: /_ChuckMiller
LinkedIn: /in/MillerChuck
Twitter: /_ChuckMiller
#ChuckMiller

LOOKING FOR MORE?

The companion website to *Discovering Love Online: Love May Be Closer Than You Think* provides supplementary materials to assist you in the search for the love of your life. Access is free, so please take advantage of all it has to offer. Available tools and resources include…

♥ A blog that contains a growing collection of useful articles that expand on the book's content.

♥ Reviews of products and services that cover related topics beyond the scope of the book.

♥ A monthly newsletter designed to inform you when new content is added.

♥ A regularly updated list of promotions and discounts offered by the major online dating services.

♥ First access to new *Discovering Love Online* products when they become available.

VISIT THE WEBSITE AT

DISCOVERINGLOVEONLINE♥COM

NOTES

PREFACE

[1]A hyperlink is an embedded reference to data stored in another location—a file, whole document or a specific element within a document—that a reader can access directly by clicking, tapping or hovering over it.

[2]Informally referred to as a web address, a URL (Uniform Resource Locator) is a protocol for specifying where a webpage or file can be located on the Internet.

[3]https://discoveringloveonline.com/online-dating-resources.

[4]https://discoveringloveonline.com/blog.

[5]https://discoveringloveonline.com/love-notes.

[6]https://discoveringloveonline.com/internet-dating-survey.

[7]https://www.facebook.com/discoveringloveonline.

[8]https://www.facebook.com/groups/discoveringloveonline.

⁹https://www.instagram.com/discoveringloveonline.

¹⁰https://twitter.com/discoverloveon.

¹¹https://www.bauerleadership.com.

¹²http://doodlemachine.com.

¹³https://cherryblossomphotography.org.

¹⁴https://discoveringloveonline.com/eharmony.

INTRODUCTION

[1]"Online Dating Statistics," *Statistic Brain Research Institute*, May 12, 2017, http://www.statisticbrain.com/online-dating-statistics.

[2]John T. Cacioppo, "Marital satisfaction and break-ups differ across on-line and off-line meeting venues," *PNAS Online*, May 1, 2013, http://www.pnas.org/content/110/25/10135.full.

CHAPTER ONE: START WITH THE BASICS

[1]1 Corinthians 7:28.

[2]Genesis 2:18.

[3]"Married People Less Likely to Have Cardiovascular Problems, According to Large-Scale Study by Researchers at NYU Langone," *NYU Langone Health*, March 28, 2014, https://discoveringloveon line.com/langone.

[4]1 Corinthians 7:35.

[5]1 Corinthians 7:7.

[6]Romans 8:28.

[7]https://www.divorcecare.org.

[8]https://www.griefshare.org.

[9]Alexander Pope, "An Essay on Criticism," *Poetry Foundation*, October 13th, 2009, https://discoveringloveonline.com/pope.

[10]https://discoveringloveonline.com/filling-the-void-of-the-soul.

[11]Andy Stanley, *The New Rules for Love, Sex, and Dating* (Grand Rapids: Zondervan, 2014), 206.

[12]While this quotation has been attributed to Albert Einstein, no evidence exists to confirm he actually said it. Others who have been credited as its source include Benjamin Franklin, Mark Twain and mystery writer Rita Mae Brown.

[13]Google Search, referred to commonly as Google, is the world's most-used Internet search engine. As such, its name has become synonymous with the search process. Thus, to "google" refers to conducting a web-based search. Just don't confuse googling with giggling. Although, the former can frequently cause the latter.

CHAPTER TWO: CHOOSE THE BEST SERVICE

[1]Proverbs 18:22 MSG.

[2]Marisa Meltzer, "Online Dating: Match Me If You Can," *Consumer Reports*, December 29, 2016, https://discoveringloveonline.com/matchme.

[3]https://www.jdate.com.

[4]https://www.catholicmatch.com.

[5]If you discover any inaccuracies in the descriptions of the dating services covered or the features offered, please send corrections to contact@discoveringloveonline.com. Thank you!

CHAPTER THREE: PUT SAFETY FIRST

[1]"Online Dating & Relationships," *Pew Research Center*, October 21, 2013, https://discoveringloveonline.com/relationships.

[2]https://mail.google.com.

[3]https://mail.yahoo.com.

[4]https://voice.google.com.

[5]"Consumer Sentinel Network Data Book for January–December 2016," *FTC*, March 2017, https://discoveringloveonline.com/data.

[6]"Sweetheart Swindle: Avoiding an Online Dating Scam," *Consumer Reports*, December 29, 2016, https://discoveringloveonline.com/scam.

[7]https://discoveringloveonline.com/mace.

[8]https://www.google.com.

[9]https://www.facebook.com.

[10]https://www.linkedin.com.

[11]https://www.instagram.com.

[12]https://www.intelius.com.

[13]https://images.google.com.

[14]https://www.tineye.com.

[15]Matthew 7:7.

CHAPTER FOUR: CREATE A WINNING PROFILE

[1]While this quote is attributed to Oscar Wilde, no evidence exists to that effect. The earliest known use appeared anonymously in 1999 and shortly thereafter it was credited to Gilbert Perreira.

[2]Attributed to many individuals, including Benjamin Franklin, Sir Edwin Sandys and William Shakespeare, the first documented occurrence of this phrase appeared in the book *Don Quixote* written by the Spanish novelist Miguel de Cervantes Saavedra, Chapter 33, translated by Pierre Antoine Motteux.

[3]The lapidary arts consist of cutting, grinding and polishing stone, minerals and gems into decorative items and jewelry. In short, it's the art of cutting or forming gemstones.

[4]Alexander Todorov and Jenny M. Porter, "Misleading First Impressions," *Psychological Science* Vol 25, Issue 7, May 27, 2014, https://discoveringloveonline.com/misleading.

[5]Allison Braley, "The 5 Minute Guide to Building the Perfect Online Dating Profile," *The Date Mix*, December 30, 2013, https://discoveringloveonline.com/5minute.

[6]"New Research Study Breaks Down 'The Perfect Profile Photo,'" *Photofeeler*, May 13, 2014, https://blog.photofeeler.com/perfect-photo.

CHAPTER SIX: IMPROVE COMMUNICATION SKILLS

[1]An indefinable, elusive quality that makes someone distinctive or attractive.

[2]Kelly Cooper, "A Woman's Advantage," *The OkCupid Blog*, March 5, 2015, https://discoveringloveonline.com/advantage.

[3]http://www.16software.com/breevy.

[4]https://textexpander.com.

[5]http://www.ergonis.com/products/typinator.

CHAPTER EIGHT: GET TO THE HEART OF THE MATTER

[1] 1 Peter 3:8.

[2] 1 Corinthians 13:4-7.

[3] Ephesians 5:1-2.

[4] Romans 12:10.

[5] Proverbs 13:12.

[6] Genesis 2:18–25.

[7] Acts 15:29, 1 Corinthians 7:2, 8-9 and 1 Thessalonians 4:3.

[8] 1 Corinthians 6:19.

[9] 1 Corinthians 7:4.

[10] 1 Corinthians 13:4-7.

[11] Bill Hendrick, "Benefits in Delaying Sex Until Marriage," *WebMD*, December 28, 2010, https://discoveringloveonline.com/delaying.

[12] Jeremiah 29:11.

CHAPTER NINE: NEVER GIVE UP

[1] Marisa Meltzer, "Online Dating: Match Me If You Can," *Consumer Reports*, December 29, 2016, https://discoveringloveonline.com/matchme.

CHAPTER TEN: CONFIRM IT'S A MATCH

[1] 1 Corinthians 13:4-8.

[2] A test which has only two outcomes, positive or negative.

[3] https://discoveringloveonline.com/before-you-save-the-date.

EPILOGUE

[1]Proverbs 16:9 NLT.

[2]Richard and Linda Eyre, *Life Balance*, (New York: Ballantine Books, 1987), 101.

POSTSCRIPT

[1]https://discoveringloveonline.com/book.

[2]http://www.andrejolicoeur.com.

AUTHOR BIO

[1]https://propellercap.com.

70621203R00099

Made in the USA
Middletown, DE
15 April 2018